A Guide to Academic Writing

A Guide to Academic Writing

JEFFREY A. CANTOR

PRAEGER

Westport, Connecticut
London

Library of Congress Cataloging-in-Publication Data

Cantor, Jeffrey A.
   A guide to academic writing / Jeffrey A. Cantor.
      p.   cm.
   Includes bibliographical references and index.
   ISBN 0-275-94660-6 (alk. paper)
   1. Authorship.   2. Authors and publishers.   3. Scholarly
publishing.   I. Title.
   PN146.C33   1993b
   808'.02—dc20   93-564

British Library Cataloguing in Publication Data is available.

A hardcover edition of *A Guide to Academic Writing* is available from the Greenwood
Press imprint of Greenwood Publishing Group, Inc.
(ISBN 0-313-29017-2)

Library of Congress Catalog Card Number: 93-564
ISBN: 0-275-94660-6

First published in 1993

Praeger Publishers, 88 Post Road West, Westport, CT 06881
An imprint of Greenwood Publishing Group, Inc.

Printed in the United States of America

The paper used in this book complies with the
Permanent Paper Standard issued by the National
Information Standards Organization (Z39.48–1984).

10 9 8 7 6 5 4 3 2 1

Copyright Acknowledgment

Extract reprinted from *How to Write and Publish a Scientific Paper, 3rd Edition*
by Robert A. Day. Published by The Oryx Press. Copyright 1988 by Robert
A. Day. Reproduced by permission of Robert A. Day and The Oryx Press.

Contents

Figures and Tables

FIGURES

TABLES

Preface

Undoubtedly the most common topic of discussion among new academics is the requirement for publication. Getting published is essential to a successful career in higher education. Likewise, the seasoned professor, contemplating promotion and/or prominence in the field, often wishes to branch out into new kinds of publication ventures. Professionals in an organization allied to the academic institution also seek information about competing in the academic publications arena.

To all of these needs this book is addressed. As a handbook on academic publishing, the work is intended to provide basic information on getting into academic print. I have approached academic publishing from the traditional academic triangle. I consider the contributions of work in the classroom to be publishable material. Service-based accomplishments such as consultation and speeches also merit consideration for potential writing and publication. And, of course, research and general scholarship contribute to our ability to publish. The book addresses the why's and how's of developing publishable manuscripts based upon an individual scholar's likes and accomplishments in each of these service areas.

Chapters treat the mechanics of producing articles for scholarly journals, conference papers, and successful grant writing to support academic activities. There are also individual chapters describing scholarly, text, and trade book publications.

I believe you will find this book interesting and useful.

Acknowledgments

Researching and writing a book of this kind is no easy task. When it is completed, it represents a team effort of tremendous proportions. I would like to acknowledge and thank the members of the team for making this an enjoyable and productive effort. First, and foremost is my wife, Ruth Cantor. She is a unique and valuable collaborator, facilitator, and motivator. She also single-handedly performed the data entry, manuscript preparation, proofreading, and bibliographic cataloging. She is a real partner. My son, David E. Cantor, proved his computer science skills through graphic support and allied research into areas of electronic data retrieval and electronic manuscript preparation.

I would also like to thank Mr. John T. Harney, who at the commencement of this project was editorial director of Auburn House. Mr. Harney provided the opportunity to launch this project, and the support to see it through completion.

Chapter 1

A Guide to Academic Writing

This book is a general guide to help you succeed in academic writing. *Successful* academic writers have definite purposes for writing. They know why they are writing and what publishing can do for their careers. As Henson (1987) has stated, "This clarity of purpose for writing provides authors with energy, drive, and persistence—qualities that lend to success" (p. 8).

As college professors, we frequently think about writing. We may want to contribute to the advancement of our profession and as experts in a field write to share ideas and research findings. We may write to attain promotion or to open opportunities for a better academic position. The more senior may write for fun and profit—publishing royalties.

The most pressure-laden reason for writing is the so-called publish-or-perish pressure that pervades most university campuses. The research and publication reward model still has a strong grip on higher education (Soderberg, 1985). No matter what one's motivation, successful writing requires specific strategies for deciding what to write and where to publish.

WHY THIS GUIDE

Many in academic careers do not have a sound understanding of or experience in publishing fundamentals. University academic preparation programs often fail to provide this training. Many faculty are unsure of what constitutes an appropriate and sufficient publication basis for tenure or promotion. This guide is, accordingly, meant to fulfill the need for information about publishing and the ways and means to achieve academic publication.

The Politics of Publication

Colleges and universities generally favor an academic triangle when judging academic performance (see Smith, 1990). Although this consists of three components, research and publication are clearly weighed more heavily than teaching and service. A successful publication record is frequently the most important factor in determining tenure, promotion, and, on occasion, merit pay. Studies over the last decade have documented that publications are essential to tenure and promotion.

The American university is undergoing a period of revision involving a renewed emphasis on the classroom (Smith, 1990; Cheney, 1990). While the emphasis on research and publication is not likely to cease, what will probably emerge is a renewed interest in teaching and the instructional technique. Writing about activity taking place in the classroom may well be a natural extension of this change. The ability to integrate classroom practice with writing and publication will undoubtedly be weighed more favorably than in the past. More writing opportunities will be available to those faculty who fully participate in teaching, research, and service (the full academic triangle); therefore, the possibility of successful publishing should increase. A relationship between the academic triangle and publishing success is thus formed and strengthened. This guide is approached from that philosophical viewpoint.

THE POLITICS OF ACADEMIA

What to Publish and What Gets Published

To ease anxiety levels regarding whether a work will be accepted for publication, Chapter 2 discusses the political considerations of what and where to publish and why. To place writing and publication in perspective, Chapter 2 discusses important academic political issues and considerations. Discussion centers on analyzing past accomplishments and present activities in light of what is valued at a college or university for making tenure and promotion decisions. The chapter poses food for thought, stimulating a review of personal academic activities and planning a course of action for successful research and writing.

Analyzing Individual Academic Activities. Pre-tenure faculty have already engaged in professional activities that can lay a foundation for a successful publishing career. The new Ph.D. has developed research and writing skills as demonstrated by the dissertation. Dissertation research can itself become a first step to an initial refereed publication or conference paper. New faculty often want to develop an article or two based upon this original research. I will address the process through which a dissertation can be reworked into a publishable article or scholarly book.

Develop a Personal Plan of Action. Pre-tenure faculty publication plans differ from those of senior faculty. Most tenure committees prefer publication in refereed journals. Other, less rigorous media (i.e., in-house publications, college-based periodicals, conferences) might, however, be a good place to try out new ideas (see CUNY, 1990; Luey, 1990). What about alternative routes? Many faculty regularly attend conferences or symposia. Can these activities lead to publication? Pre-tenure faculty should consider personal interests, talents, and available resources in order to formulate a plan of action. The academic triangle's requirements, as the baseline for tenure and promotion decision making, can be met through planning and a course of action.

For example, as a social scientist in the training and development field, I maintain a research agenda focusing on training and development policy research. I support it with federal and state grants. These funds provide an opportunity to conduct research using student research assistants. I use the research data to write. New knowledge and information are disseminated through several media: (1) publishing in professional refereed research based journals, trade journals, and professional conferences; (2) consulting to business and industry to provide new directions based on this new information; (3) presentations to other academics and professionals; and (4) teaching. The research also provides students with opportunities to work, learn, and explore their academic interests. I have been able to meet professional obligations through a plan of action constructed around my research interests.

Understanding the forces that are at work when a panel of referees decides whether or not a manuscript gets into print can also be helpful when selecting a journal. Chapter 2 provides an overview of these various avenues for publication—including scholarly journals and books, conference and symposium papers, trade books, and electronic media.

Information Is Power: Resources Are Available

One may browse the library's shelves reviewing indexes and journals: assessing the kinds of articles published, academic writing styles, and editorial policies of a journal. Look at the organization (university press or professional association) sponsoring a journal, and names and locations of contributors to the particular media. Often insights into topics to write, or opportunities for writing, or collaborations can be identified. Chapter 3 provides information about available research tools which can help make publishing more successful. This chapter describes indexes, periodicals, and serials, directories, and reference holdings typical of a collegiate library. These resources support writing and publishing activities and assist in identification of various publishing opportunities. Adequate reference materials are invaluable for assisting a publishing career. It is increasingly essential to understand computer-assisted data identification and retrieval. Chapter 3 will describe these kinds of resources as well.

Pre-tenure faculty often agonize until they place their first publication. For them, or those in non-university-based positions, Chapters 4 and 6 describe developing and directing manuscripts for refereed journals and professional conferences.

Writing for Professional Journals

The most powerful and best recognized scholarly publishing medium, as indicated by all of the studies cited herein, is the refereed journal. Chapter 4 is a guide to refereed journal publishing. Included are suggestions for identifying and selecting an appropriate journal, gathering preliminary information about manuscript preparation for that journal, and writing and developing the manuscript. A refereed journal is a publication which is supervised and directed by academicians or professionals in a specific field or discipline. The decision to publish a manuscript as an article is decided by a "blind" review committee consisting of three to five (depending on the journal) referees. These referees do not know the name of the author of the manuscript they are reading. Thus, the review should be made fairly, and judged solely on its academic merits. Refereed journals are usually university-based, managed and edited by academicians, and supported by professional associations and/or university stipends. Chapter 4 also describes the preparation of manuscripts.

Chapter 5 provides more information on journal article writing. It addresses such considerations as galley proofs and copyright issues. The chapter also discusses participation in journal article reviews and service as a journal referee. Chapter 5 also contains useful information on the growing medium of electronic journals. The chapter discusses identifying and accessing electronic journals and submitting material through computer interface networks.

Conference/Symposium Papers and Presentations

Chapter 6 describes procedures for identifying and selecting appropriate organizations for which to write and present conference papers. A conference paper affords both pre-tenure faculty members and seasoned scholars a viable means to communicate ideas to others and to gain constructive criticism. Luey (1990) and others suggest that a very good way to test material for refereed journals is the refereed conference paper. One may, of course, develop a scholarly article from a conference paper. In addition, many organizations publish their conference proceedings. This chapter also focuses on the best ways to develop and present a conference paper and follow it through to publication.

Sponsored/Funded Research Activities: Developing Grants and Contracts

Chapter 7 is devoted to writing and developing grant proposals. It provides tested and proven procedures for developing sound funding proposals. Many faculty use grants to support their research activities. Grant funds may also make the difference in getting a manuscript into print, especially when subventions are required. The chapter describes how to identify funding opportunities, how to obtain information from grants sources, and how to write responsive proposals.

Scholarly Books, Texts, and Monographs

Chapters 8 to 10 deal with the specifics of book writing and publishing, including electronic publishing. Chapter 11 is devoted to marketing texts. These chapters provide insights into book and monograph publishing from a three-phase perspective: (1) pre-contractual considerations—including identifying a topic and publisher—and book prospectus development; (2) contract negotiations and the mechanics of manuscript development; and (3) marketing and book promotion. The scholarly book and/or monograph is highly valued by all faculty. It is often a requirement for promotion.

Scholarly Books. Chapter 8 describes pre-contractual considerations for the writing of scholarly books and monographs and textbooks. Like refereed journals, scholarly book publishers use a peer review process to qualify appropriate scholarly work for publication. However, because of tight markets, decreases in sales of scholarly books (a typical book may sell between 500 and 1,000 copies), and rising printing costs, academic presses have become very selective about what they print. University presses are revising their role in the academic publishing market, in large part as a result of a decline in some traditional sales areas, the economy, and cultural change. Electronic publishing is also a major factor in decreased use and sales of paper print products (Coughlin, 1991). Therefore, careful planning and writing, followed by astute publisher contact and interface, are necessary to place a manuscript successfully.

Textbooks. The textbook is also a publishing accomplishment in some fields. Textbook publications include elementary and high school (EL-HI) and college texts and related materials. Chapter 9 treats college text and reference book publishing, and Chapter 10 discusses elementary and high school publications (EL-HI publishing). A well received textbook can be highly financially rewarding for the writer, but the textbook market is also highly competitive. Chapter 9 also presents information about electronic manuscript preparation, including available software, disk formatting, and script layout.

Chapter 10 concludes with some information on author supported vanity presses and self-publishing of books and other media. While neither vanity presses nor self-publishing is viewed as scholarly, this information is provided to illustrate available options. Computer software is also discussed. Trade or general book publishing is also briefly discussed in Chapter 8. A non-fiction trade book offers entertainment or general information appropriate to a wide audience. Each publishing segment offers exciting challenges for the academician.

Emerging Opportunities

Chapter 11 discusses book marketing, which is the last phase of the book publication process. The chapter suggests basic steps in publicity, promotion, and commercial sales and assists you in following the marketplace progress of your work.

Successful academic writers generally enjoy writing and the related publishing activity. It is my hope that this book will assist others in that experience.

REFERENCES

Cheney, L. V. (1990). Research and teaching: An excerpt from Cheney report on educational practices gone wrong. *The Chronicle of Higher Education*, November 14, *37*(9), A22, 24–26.

Coughlin, E. K. (1991). University presses ponder their role in a future clouded by financial and cultural upheaval. *The Chronicle of Higher Education*, July, A5, A9.

CUNY Faculty Development Program. (1990). *On publishing in the academia*. New York: New York Professional Staff Congress/CUNY.

Henson, K. T. (1987). *Writing for professional publication*. Bloomington IN: Phi Delta Kappa Educational Foundation.

Luey, B. (1990). *Handbook for academic authors*. Cambridge, England: Cambridge University Press.

Smith, P. (1990). *Killing the spirit: Higher education in America*. New York: Viking Penguin.

Soderberg, L. O. (1985). Dominance of research and publication: An unrelenting tyranny. *College Teaching*, Fall, *33*(4), 168–172.

Chapter 2

The Politics of Academic Publishing: Setting a Personal Course of Action

The university is a political institution. Publishing for reappointment with tenure and/or promotion is often as much a political process as an intellectual one. Norms affecting the kinds of publishing that receive recognition differ from university to university. Changing demands on the academic institution, especially the debate over teaching versus research, affect promotion and tenure committees' collective perceptions of publication accomplishments. Committee makeup also affects perceptions of a given professor's accomplishments, and administrators' opinions and votes likewise vary. It is important, accordingly, to learn in detail about the criteria, including publications, on which one will be judged.

WHAT TO PUBLISH

Where does one begin? This chapter describes the following steps:

1. Determining what is valued at a college or university
2. Analyzing individual academic activities and accomplishments
3. Developing a personal plan of action

What Is Valued at Your University

The Promotion and Tenure Committee. Most tenure and promotion decision making originates at the academic department level. A promotion and tenure committee at this level will probably have the most influence on a pre-tenure faculty member's career. It is, again, important to find out about any publications criteria by which one may be judged. There may be no printed guidelines outlining such criteria; yet discussion will yield the feelings and perceptions of the present committee membership—which often do not change dramatically over an extended period.

Several studies on faculty tenure and promotion have been conducted over the past decade. Schweitzer (1989) presents data which reflect many of these other studies. This survey of administrators suggests that non-tenured faculty who prefer teaching to research and who hope to get past tenure and promotion committees through "continuing professional achievement" may be in danger of being passed over (p. 45). Table 2-1 presents some of the Schweitzer study findings. Euster and Weinbach (1986) also found that refereed journal publications and scholarly books were ranked highest in deans' favor for tenure and promotion.

There is little disagreement among these administrators that the most important activity of a faculty member is writing a scholarly book. Faculty in undergraduate (baccalaureate) degree granting colleges may receive more credit than their university colleagues for activities such as reviewing

Table 2-1
Factors Considered Most Important When Evaluating Faculty for Promotion and/or Tenure by Highest Degree Offered

Factor	Overall Mean	Highest Degree Offered		
		Bachelors	Masters	Doctorate
Classroom Teaching*	3.83	3.88	3.88	3.63
Publication*	3.44	3.19	3.46	3.84
Research*	3.33	3.00	3.46	3.63
Service	3.16	3.25	3.19	2.95
Student Advising	3.10	3.31	3.02	2.90
Professional Organizations	2.82	2.88	2.78	2.79
Committee Work	2.76	2.84	2.76	2.63
Length of Service	2.67	2.81	2.63	2.42
Successful Grant Applications	2.53	2.31	2.61	2.74
**Supervision of Graduate Studies	2.18	1.34	2.49	3.00

Note: * Statistically Significant at (.05).
      ** Faculty in undergraduate (B.S.) only colleges may receive more credit than their university colleagues in activities section; in reviewing for national journals; editing newsletters; and writing book reviews.

(From John C. Schweitzer, "Faculty research expectation varies among universities." Reproduced from *Journalism Educator*, Vol. 44, No. 2, Summer 1989, p. 46 with permission of the Association for Education in Journalism and Mass Communication.)

for national journals, authoring newsletters, and writing book reviews. Publication in refereed journal articles likewise will be a primary and important consideration. Articles in national magazines or non-refereed journals rank below more traditional research in importance to tenure and promotion. Determine whether certain journals (national or international) are valued more—and whether certain journals which might have emerged in a field are valued at all.

If the department committee regards only refereed journals as significant, or requires that publication be in periodicals with national reputations, you should obviously concentrate your efforts on these types of publications. For example, some committees may not view editing or collaboration as a true indicator of success in original research.

How do the committee members view conferences and symposia? What about book reviews and newsletter pieces? Popular and general publication? Many pre-tenure faculty ask about numbers of publications: Do they have some numerical standard or paper count? Usually no. While many tenure and promotion committee members claim they do not hold numbers in high regard—they usually prefer quality to quantity—one must consider the numerical values possessed by those who ultimately judge.

Departmental committee politics notwithstanding, refereed journal and scholarly book publication is most highly regarded as it reflects peer judgment. Within this category of publication scholarship, the kind of journal, quality of publication, methods of peer review, acceptance of the work by readers as evidenced by numbers of citations elsewhere, all are factors in academic politics as well.

Speak with Several Faculty Who Have Preceded You. Nothing speaks better than experience—lessons learned. Like those in any other organization, those with the keenest understanding are often the people who have had recent experience with the tenure or promotion process. What kinds of publications were accepted, and which were regarded highly?

The nature of one's discipline also affects the weighing of publication accomplishment. One refereed article in a nationally recognized journal such as the *New England Journal of Medicine* on a double-blind test and verification of a cancer-arresting drug could be enough to win tenure for an assistant professor of biochemistry at University X, whereas a dozen articles describing research and opinion of an assistant professor of education at University Y might not be sufficient.

Finally, the publishing industry is political in its own right. A faculty member seeking book publication should understand the forces affecting scholarly press and book publisher decision making. While scholarly presses operate as intellectual gatekeepers, as Parsons (1989) so aptly labels them, and theoretically consider costs and budgets after scholarship, rising costs, specialized markets, and commercial competition all affect decision making.

How can a professor deal with these factors and forces and be successful in publishing? Successful writers begin by assessing the expectations and values at the university.

Analyze Activities and Accomplishments

Consider Your Long-Range Career Goals. In the quest for a publication track record we may forget to consider our own desires and goals. We should not fall prey to this trap. Successful writers begin by searching their own desires. Through university service we have the advantage of choosing our research, within broad limits, and we should exercise this freedom. As best expressed by Shulman (1979), ''It is axiomatic that the reward system is incongruent with the real activities and interests of most faculty and the purposes of most institutions'' (p. 45). First, we must weigh our own long-term goals. Ask yourself why you chose academia as a career. What do you want to contribute? In what kinds of professional activities do you like to engage? Do you like to speak professionally? Consult? You will ultimately write best about what you best like to do.

Next, successful writers establish specific agendas for academic work. These writers define focused areas of research or inquiry. Many couple these research activities with teaching assignments. Boyes et al. (1984) cite data that indicate that research and teaching are weighted equally for tenure and promotion at colleges which grant undergraduate (bachelor's and master's) degrees and that teaching weighs more heavily at institutions that grant only the bachelor's degree.

Some set goals of both writing sponsored grants and research and conducting non-sponsored (or self-directed) research. Be motivated to write about what has been found to be useful through your research. Many successful writers make it a point to write and publish several journal articles and conference papers based on the outcome of research. Larger projects might result in scholarly book publication. However, as Adams (1989) writes:

Junior faculty are . . . encouraged to put forth (early) their best scholarly efforts . . . staking one's chances for tenure and promotion on a single opus magnus that takes years to complete is at best risky. One colleague expended so much time standardizing a test she had developed that she failed to publish the protocol before her tenure votes. (p. 56)

It is best to concentrate on smaller, high-quality publishable pieces. Later earlier research projects as well as classroom and community work can be combined in a book for publication—theory to practice!

Develop a Plan of Action

A personal plan of action should be based on the collective suggestions (values) of the college and its promotion and tenure committees, *as well as* one's own personal goals. The best way to ensure early success is to build upon past successes and accomplishments. A person who has an academic appointment has presumably demonstrated a certain professional record of achievement. This may have been a lauded dissertation, or it may have been an earlier record of writing, consultation, and teaching. In any event, past efforts should provide a foundation and a point of commencement for future writing success.

Making Dissertations Publishable. Consider using dissertation research as a first publication. Consider it a challenge to get such work published in a journal in your field and/or to present the work at a scholarly conference. Parsons (1989) offers suggestions for converting dissertations to publishable works. There is a belief that 90 percent of all doctoral dissertations are unpublishable in their research report form. Yet many very good works emanate from these beginnings. There are university and other specialized presses that seek out exemplary dissertations for a yearly series. While your dissertation may not lend itself to adaptation for a scholarly book (at least in its present state) certainly a part of it can be included in a "report of research" type of journal article. Determine who would benefit from the new information.

Regarding dissertation research, ask the following questions:

1. Does the thesis or dissertation contribute useful new knowledge of reasonably broad interest to the field?
2. Am I seriously interested in continuing to work it into a publishable form?
3. Does the university promotion and tenure committee see the subject material as a potentially valuable work for publication?
4. What journals or conferences are appropriate media for the subject?
5. Can I envision a future research agenda based upon my dissertation research?
6. Can I relate my research findings to a current problem, situation, or area of personal interest?
7. Do I know a publisher's essential requirements?

Reviews of Literature. Another avenue for the pre-tenure faculty member is the review of literature and/or book reviews. Some faculty merge a dissertation into a line of research inquiry by synthesizing it with existing literature in a field of study, to produce a meta-analytic study. This kind of activity facilitates development of publishable material into an agenda for further research.

Other activities might include the following:

- Teaching assignments and student research and theses
- Speeches, community work, even sermons
- Conference paper presentations
- Consulting and research
- Grant writing

Teaching Assignments. Much national attention has been focused upon teaching in the university (see Cheney report, 1990). This concern is causing university leadership to direct more attention to a pre-tenure faculty member's accomplishments in the classroom. Areas of curriculum development, instructional innovations, and special teaching methods now are legitimate grounds for publication. Activities might include expanding a special syllabus into a textbook. Some faculty use a personal philosophical argument as the impetus for a new method of teaching of a subject and as the basis for articles. Or one may develop and write about new kinds of teacher preparation, course development, or instructional processes. These ideas can be developed into a series of articles for journals and newsletters, letters to the editor, and/or debates in journals. Often these projects act as a catalyst for student follow-on research.

Speeches and Community Work. Many college professors are invited to speak before civic, professional, or other community groups. Some are involved in religious or political activities. Many of these activities present opportunities for writing.

Conference Presentations. Opportunities for publication also result from participation in conferences, symposia, and seminars. Many of us are inspired by presentations made by others, ideas advanced in debates, or critiques of papers presented. Oftentimes, we can cowrite a paper based on a common theme with one or two other presenters. We also network through conferences and symposia and learn of journals which deal with some of the topics about which we have an interest in writing.

Sponsors of conferences and symposia look for submissions which represent unique contributions of interest to the organization. Usually these are reports of research findings with specific messages containing innovative contributions to the field. They may be philosophical issues, roundtable discussions, or symposia sessions led by the contributor and designed to provide a forum for understanding or dealing with the topic. In any event, organizers of conferences suggest that participants should have well developed contributions to make. Faculty members seeking to broaden their writing scope often use conferences to network and determine the publishability of their material and the peculiarities of specific organizationally sponsored journals.

Consulting and Research. Consulting and sponsored research can also offer excellent opportunities to publish. Many of the topics we write about arise in consulting work. We write about the projects, as well as opportunities to extend their results into the academic world or classroom. Many faculty write journal articles and conference papers on aspects of the work that are unique and contribute to the discipline: some of the work may relate to classroom teaching. Faculty often develop very publishable material through these experiences. Successful authors write about topics which are fresh or new. Sponsored research offers special opportunities to publish work under the aegis of established organizations (more about this in Chapter 7).

Grant Writing. Part of academic writing is grant writing to support research. Promotion and tenure committees look favorably on development and writing of grant proposals—especially those successfully funded. Consider grant writing as you make decisions about a personal writing agenda.

NOW GET STARTED

It is a truism that getting started is always the most difficult part of a writing effort. Faculty often complain that they cannot find enough time to write and teach concurrently. However, the fact is that publishing is an important part of an academic career, and therefore it is important to make and budget time. Set goals, manageable ones, and meet them. Set a goal such as "outline the first section of the manuscript this week." And then follow through.

Penaskovic offers several survival skills for scholarly writers which can help one get started:

- First, get motivated and avoid procrastination. A successful writer will write out a list of writing tasks to do each day and then adhere to that list. Make use of professional memberships—conferences and symposia —as "an excuse" to develop a paper which can lead to a journal manuscript.
- Second, keep an eye out for opportunities to write—such as consultancies, research conducted or in progress, and teaching situations. Think about things happening in the field—philosophical slants worth writing about.
- Be original and present only new information and fresh insights. Some authors bring new insights to old ideas or concepts; some introduce new data; and still others provide up-to-date reviews of the field. All of these approaches can work well.
- Set up a writing schedule that capitalizes on a work or teaching schedule and personal work habits.
- Work out a draft. Get something down on paper. Draft ideas on a word processor, then edit—add, rework, or revise. Do not worry about

polishing each stage of material when working on a draft. Before long, a manuscript will begin to appear.

Ideas become cleaner and more workable when put on paper. Many academics write to think. We think better when we can see in print our thoughts and concepts. We can play with them on paper. We can have others critique and review them as well. Begin writing!

Avoid Common Errors When Attempting to Publish

In the following chapters you will be given some insights and hints for avoiding some of the more common writing errors. What are these common errors?

Ignorance of Publication Requirements of Journal Publishers or Conference Sponsors. One of the major mistakes people make when attempting to publish is neglecting to find out the writing requirements and styles (including manuscript preparation conventions) of the particular journals. The solution is simple: secure and carefully review copies of a few editions of the journal before submitting a manuscript for publication consideration. Request a copy of the journal's style or requirements sheet.

Stylistic Writing Problems. Note whether the particular journal uses first person versus third person pronouns. If graphics appear in the journal, how are they used? Does the journal stress technical versus philosophical pieces?

Basic Grammar. Nothing disaffects a journal editor or a reviewer more than the need to correct spelling and grammatical errors found in a manuscript. Such lapses quickly discourage reviewers from concentrating on the manuscript's content and substance. Many manuscripts are ultimately rejected because of basic grammatical and format errors. Standard academic writing guides should be reviewed and referred to as necessary in the course of writing.

Excessive Verbiage. Many manuscripts tend to verbosity. Readers and publishers appreciate works that are well planned and concisely stated. It is important to draft the manuscript, review, condense, rewrite, incorporate any illustrative material, and ask informed friends and colleagues to read and react to the work. It is sometimes helpful to have a person who does not work in the field, perhaps a spouse, read the work.

Overuse of Academic Jargon. Our various disciplines tend to overuse, if not invent, academic jargon. Journal editors have become sensitive to distractions which affect readability of an article when such language is used. Most editors stress the limitation, elimination, or careful use of specialized vocabulary or jargon. Define carefully all such terminology. Use common language and terms if at all possible.

Poor Use of Graphics. Graphics are often important in complex technical writing. Do not, however, try to be the professional illustrator unless you are truly an expert. Buy or draft this talent. Likewise tables, charts, and even illustrations help. Be alert to the publisher's requirements for reproduction.

OK, So What If I Do All This, Write an Article, and Get Rejected?

Keep the Faith. Manuscripts do, of course, frequently come back with negative publishing decisions. Consider and, when appropriate, capitalize on the reviewer's and editor's comments and rewrite. Authors will sometimes resubmit a reworked manuscript to a journal or begin writing for another. Many decide on a list of journals to which they will submit a manuscript—in descending order—rewriting and submitting as each makes a "not-to-accept" decision.

Some manuscripts are accepted as submitted—sometimes with very minor changes; some are conditionally accepted pending a rewrite with specific changes; others are rejected with an invitation for a rewrite and redevelopment. In this case, the journal is interested in the topic but not satisfied with the writing style and development of the manuscript. Another possibility is a rejection with no invitation for readmission. Here the topic may be inappropriate or the writing quality such that the editor is not willing to work with it. In most cases either blind copies of the reviewer findings or a summary by the editor of the findings—or both—are enclosed.

Editorial response is important in redeveloping the manuscript. If it is not provided, consider calling the editor and requesting specific comments. Sometimes they can be provided; in other instances, no further comments will be forthcoming. Do not give up on a manuscript once you write it. Rewrite it, polish it, and submit it to another journal. Publishing decisions are highly subjective.

Chapter 3 provides information about research tools and using them to identify publishing opportunities. The sources of information are plentiful. The chapter highlights specific sources of publication information, usually in college and university (as well as most public) libraries.

REFERENCES

Adams, M. R. (1989). Tenuring and promoting junior faculty. *Thought and Action*, Fall 5(2), 35–60.

Boyes, W. J., Happel, S. K., & Hogan, T. D. (1984) Publish or perish: Fact or fiction? *Journal of Economics Education*, Spring, 136–141.

Cheney, L. V. (1990). Research and teaching: An excerpt from Cheney report on educational practices gone wrong. *The Chronicle of Higher Education*, November 14, 37(9), A22, 24–26.

Euster, G. L., & Weinbach, R. W. (1986). Deans' quality assessment of faculty
    publications for tenure and promotion decisions. *Journal of Social Work
    Education*, Fall, 22(3), 79–84.
Parsons, P. (1989). *Getting published: The acquisition process at university presses.*
    Knoxville: The University of Tennessee Press.
Penaskovic, R. (1983). Facing up to the publication gun. *Scholarly Publishing*,
    January, 136–140.
Schweitzer, J. C. (1989). Faculty research expectations vary among universities.
    Educator, Summer, 45–49.
Shulman, C. (1979). *Old expectations, new realities: The academic profession revised*
    (AAHE/ERIC Higher Education Research Report No. 2). Washington, DC:
    American Association for Higher Education.

Chapter 3

The Writing Process: Devising a Framework for Planning, Researching, and Developing a Manuscript

Scholarly writing requires a framework for planning, researching, and developing a manuscript. This chapter presents the tools which support the three phases. A concise annotated list of useful research tools and sources to plan each phase is given. This chapter also discusses the procedures for computer-aided literature searches.

PLANNING THE WRITING PROJECT

Successful writers will undoubtedly agree that their most fruitful efforts began with clear ideas about their selected topics and intended audiences. Appropriate questions such as the following are often posed.

- "What expertise do I have to share?"
- "With whom do I wish to share it?" (the audience)
- "What is the best medium through which to do so?"(journals, books, conference papers)

Consider Your Expertise

The discussion in Chapter 2 centered on personal soul searching for appropriate ideas and knowledge to share through writing. Authors must also ensure that they have a full and comprehensive knowledge of the current state of the literature in the area about which they are writing. Referee panels usually insist on comprehensive reviews of the literature, thus ensuring that the new material is discussed, described, analyzed, composed, or contrasted within an existing body of knowledge.

Perhaps the best way to finalize a topic to write about is to stay abreast of your professional surroundings. Writers read extensively. They keep up with journals in their field, as well as allied fields. They attend conferences. They get onto a computer bulletin board in their field and share ideas and essays with others. They serve as referees or editors of journals and newsletters. They dialogue with students. They avoid trendy topics because these topics often wane in interest before manuscripts get into print as articles or books. In short, they are in touch with their environment. From these varied sources comes food for thought for writing.

Identify Your Audience

With whom will you be sharing your knowledge? Are these readers colleagues in the discipline? Students? General readers? Audience issues will influence writing style. Good writers recognize the writing style requirements appropriate to an audience.

General Reference Books. There are some very good books which will aid writers to tune a manuscript's tone and language to its intended audience. Each of these should be kept close at hand when developing a manuscript.

A Handbook for Scholars by Mary Claire Van Leunen (Oxford University Press, 1992). This is a comprehensive guide to scholarly writing mechanics. It includes reference styles, footnoting, styling, format, and related issues.

Writing for Professional Publication by Kenneth T. Henson (Phi Delta Kappa Educational Foundation, 1987). This small "fastback" discusses some basics for getting a writing project off to a good start.

The Chicago Manual of Style (The University of Chicago Press, 1982). This is a general manual of style used for academic and professional writing. It is recognized as a standard reference tool for authors, copy editors, and proofreaders.

The Writer's Essential Desk Reference edited by Glenda Tennant Neff (Writer's Digest Books, 1991). This reference contains chapters on the mechanics of research and manuscript preparation. The book provides information about writing a manuscript, carrying it through publishing, and marketing a work.

RESEARCH TOOLS

There are several categories of research tools regularly used for research purposes: (1) indexes and abstracts which publish large volumes of research information (periodical indexes provide a concise and efficient guide to these published media); (2) periodicals and serials—hard-copy journals, newspapers, and other regularly published media held in a library; (3) general and specialized directories; and (4) general reference documents (including government publications). Each of these sources of information can be accessed and searched in hard copy or by computerized services. The remainder of this chapter provides guidance on using research tools to support writing projects.

Browse the Library to Identify Publication Opportunities

The library is at the center of a writing project. While we are all familiar with its holdings and services, this discussion establishes a framework for thinking about the services as they relate to manuscript development. Decisions are often gained through experience and exposure to the various media. As we look through journals for data to support a research activity, we also evaluate them as potential sources for a manuscript's submission. The stages of manuscript development may, accordingly, overlap with research for a writing project.

Browse the holdings and subscriptions contained in the journals and periodicals section. Review journals for applicability to your writing interests. Some universities house or sponsor a journal, and some faculty on the campus may be editors of journals. Valuable sources are frequently close at hand.

A useful and accessible basic source of publication opportunity is the weekly newspaper *The Chronicle of Higher Education. The Chronicle* contains up-to-date information on (1) new journals in print, (2) new scholarly books in print with publishers' addresses, (3) calls for papers, (4) announcements of conferences and symposia, (5) publisher requests for manuscripts, (6) information on sources of grants and fellowships, (7) general information on new software, and (8) trends and practices in publishing in academia. New information is printed weekly in each of these categories.

A professor in search of a scholarly publisher might review several back issues of *The Chronicle of Higher Education*'s "New Scholarly Books" section. For example, a particular publisher is active in economics and political science, among other disciplines. Knowing this, a professor in these areas might make an initial contact with the responsible editor to discuss submission of a prospectus.

DEVELOPMENT OF A WRITING PROJECT

Planning a Search

Once the writing topic is formulated and a publishing medium is identified, a literature search can begin. Knowledge of the current literature in the topic area is important when writing for a journal article or book or developing a grant proposal. Conference papers, published reviews of the literature, newsletter reviews, all emanate from such literature reviews.

The planning process (see Figure 3-1) begins with a draft of the writing topic objective. Writers think of a general title, theme statement, or writing objective. From this statement, key words or descriptors will be highlighted. For instance, for the topic objective "To describe the current practices in human performance improvement, enhancement, and evaluation in the nuclear power, chemical, and allied critical skills industries," keywords or descriptors are *performance enhancement, performance improvement, evaluation of human performance, critical-skills industries, nuclear power training, chemical industry training,* and *nuclear power safety.*

Use a Computer to Search Data. An increasing amount of information can be searched and identified electronically. Going "on-line" to search for research in the form of articles and book citations can also identify journal titles of which you may not be aware.

On-line services and CD-ROMs (computerized compact disk storage technology) make the process easier. These automated tools quickly produce useful information.

To conduct a comprehensive search of a prospective writing topic, a writer can meet with a research librarian trained in the use of search techniques for computerized data base searches (e.g., DIALOG). The librarian will assist in compiling *descriptors,* or keywords recognizable to the data base. Descriptors relate to keywords which are entered into the data base via the abstract written for that piece. These descriptors are listed in a catalog of descriptors compiled by a search service.

Depending on the data base to be searched, descriptors vary. For instance, a very popular data base in the education and allied social science disciplines is ERIC, which is a national information center located in Washington, D.C., with sixteen clearinghouses located throughout the United States. ERIC collects, screens, organizes, and catalogues pertinent educational reports and documents. Each clearinghouse is established for a specific topic: for example, the ERIC clearinghouse on community college education is at UCLA. A monthly listing, *Current Index to Journals in Education* (CIJE), published by ERIC, contains the names and addresses of the clearinghouses, and information about periodical literature. *Resources in Education* (RIE) contains educational documents including conference paper presentations and final reports of projects. (ERIC is a source of publication for professors in education and related areas; papers are screened by a clearinghouse prior to acceptance into the data base.)

The *Thesaurus of ERIC Descriptors* can be used to search CIJE and RIE on-line (or by hand through semi-annual hard copies of these documents). Keyword descriptors recognized by ERIC are identified in this thesaurus. In the section on nuclear power critical-skills evaluation cited, ERIC descriptors (both major and minor) include the following:

Figure 3-1
Literature Search

Reviewing the Literature

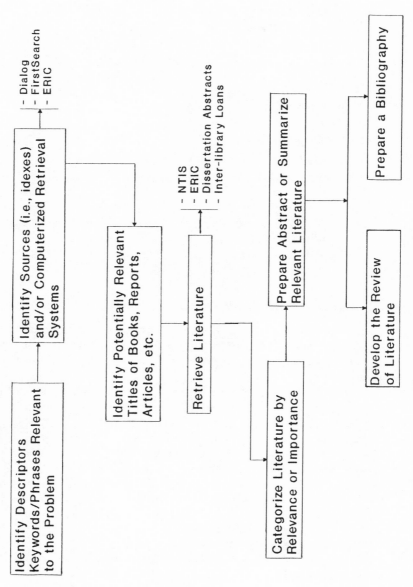

Major: Job Training
        Nuclear Power Plant Technicians
        Inservice Teacher Education
        Nuclear Technology
        Program Development
        Program Improvement

Minor: Accreditation
        Computer-Oriented Programs
        Educational Improvement
        Employee Attitudes
        Energy Occupations
        Nuclear Physics

A typical abstract produced by this search is depicted in Figure 3-2. Once relevant citations are identified, a researcher can read these abstracts on-line or print them off-line by computer. For ERIC documents, orders for the full document (fiche or hard copy) can be placed by telephone using the ERIC *Thesaurus* as a guide to a distributor.

Indexes, Directories, and Periodical Guides

There are many recognized indexes, directories, and guides to periodicals which can be useful for identifying both data for writing purposes and potential publishing opportunities. Some of these are discussed and presented in Table 3-1.

Social Sciences Index. *Social Sciences Index* is a cumulative index to English language periodicals covering 353 key international periodicals (as of December 1990). In addition to the subjects listed in Table 3-1, it indexes feature articles, review articles, scholarly replies to the literary interviews, obituaries, and biographies. *Social Sciences Index* is arranged by author and subject with all entries arranged in one listing. Title entries are not included. Articles are indexed under the surname of the author.

Social Sciences Index uses its own subject authority file, derived from the literature itself and Library of Congress subject headings. Selection of periodicals for indexing is based on subscriber preferences.

The index is guided by The Committee on Wilson Indexes of the American Library Association's Reference and Adult Services Division. The committee advises the publisher on indexing and editorial policy by conducting content studies periodically. The committee also prepares lists of periodicals representative of all subject areas which are included in the *Index*.

Applied Science & Technology Index. The *Applied Science & Technology Index* includes entries in the disciplines listed in Table 3-1. This manual is compiled

Figure 3-2
Sample Abstract

--- Record #49 ---

Accession Number: ED299381 Availability: EDRS Price - MF01/PC01 Plus Postage

AUTHOR: Gerling, Kenneth D.

TITLE: Conducting Effective Simulator Training.
YEAR: 21 Sep 88

ABSTRACT:
This paper describes the simulator phase of Commonwealth Edison's program for training and licensing operators of nuclear power stations. Topics covered include (1) preparing the students before starting the simulator phase; (2) the simulator schedule and the number of students that can be trained effectively in a class; (3) format and structure of lesson plans and drill guides for the simulator phase; (4) the evaluation tools that must be used to give candidates proper feedback on their progress; and (5) the team instruction approach. In the program described, 97 percent of the technicians being tested obtained licenses. (KC)
NOTE: Paper presented at the Midwest Nuclear Training Association Annual Nuclear Instructors" Workshop (3rd, Columbus, OH, September 21-22, 1988).

MAJOR DESCRIPTORS:
Classroom Techniques
Evaluation Methods
Job Training
Nuclear Power Plant
 Technicians
Simulation

MINOR DESCRIPTORS:
Learning Activities
Lesson Plans
Nuclear Power Plants
Outcomes of Education
Postsecondary Education
Program Evaluation
Simulated Environment
Student Evaluation

IDENTIFIERS:
Commonwealth Edison

Table 3-1
Indexes, Directories, and Periodical Guides

Index	Subjects/Contents
Social Sciences Index	Anthropology; Community Health & Medicine; Economics; Geography; International Relations; Law, Criminology & Police Science; Political Science; Psychology & Psychiatry; Public Administration; Sociology & Social Work.
Applied Science & Technology Index	Aeronautics and Space Science; Atmospheric Sciences; Chemistry; Computer Technology and applications; Construction Industry; Energy Resources and Research; Engineering, Fire and Fire Prevention; Food and Food Industry; Geology; Machinery; Mathematics; Metallurgy; Mineralogy; Oceanography; Petroleum and Gas; Physics; Plastics; Textile Industry and Fabrics; Transportation; and other Industrial and Mechanical Arts. Engineering disciplines including: Chemical; Civic; Electric and Telecommunications; Environmental; Industrial; Mining; Mechanical; and Nuclear.
Education Index	Administration and Supervision; Pre-school; Elementary; Secondary; Higher and Adult Education; Teacher Education; Vocational Education; Counseling and Personnel Service; Teaching Methods and Curriculum. Specific subject fields include: Arts, Audiovisual Education, Comparative and International Education, Computers in Education, English Language Arts; Health and Physical Education, Languages and Linguistics, Library and Information Science, Multi-Cultural/Ethnic Education, Psychology and Mental Health, Religious Education, Science and Mathematics, Social Studies, Special Education and Rehabilitation, and Educational Research relative to areas and fields indexed.
Business Periodicals Index	Accounting, Advertising and Marketing, Banking, Business and Buildings, Chemical Industry, Communications, Computer Technology and Applications, Drug and Cosmetic Industries, Economics, Electronics, Finance and Investments, Industrial Relations, Insurance, International Business Management and Personnel Management, Occupational Health and Safety, Paper and Pulp Industries, Petroleum and Gas Industries, Printing and Publishing, Public Relations, Public Utilities, Real Estate, Regulation of Industry, Transportation, and other specific business, industries, and trades.

in the same manner as the *Social Sciences Index*: Subject entries to periodical articles are arranged in one alphabetical index. There is also a separate listing of citations to book reviews.

Education Index. The *Education Index* is a cumulative index to English language educational periodicals on the subjects listed in Table 3-1. *The Education Index* is arranged in the same manner as the *Social Services Index* and the *Applied Science and Technology Index*. Note that although *Education Index* is primarily a periodical index, yearbooks and monographs are also included. There is also a separate listing of citations to book reviews.

Business Periodicals Index. Another H. W. Wilson company index is the *Business Periodicals Index*. This index covers subject fields listed in Table 3-1. A list of periodicals indexed and a list of citations to book reviews are also included in the Index. Again as a subject index, all entries are arranged in one listing.

Articles describing a company or company program are indexed under the name of the particular company. Biographical articles are indexed in another section.

Periodicals and Serials

A number of research-based companies publish abstract guides and indexes to periodicals and serials.

Ulrich's International Periodicals Directory. This directory provides a comprehensive source of accurate and complete acquisition and research information on serials. The directory lists both paperbound and hardbound editions as well as *Ulrich's Online* and *Ulrich's Plus* in CD-ROM. The twenty-seventh edition contains 108,590 titles arranged under 554 subject headings in three volumes. *Ulrich's* collects data from sixty-one thousand publishers to compile up-to-date information on new titles, title changes, and cessations. Analysis is made of publishers who do not respond to verify title cessations and publisher changes of addresses.

The twenty-seventh edition of this directory contains 10,770 brief descriptions of serials, and 16,000 Library of Congress Classification Numbers. Highlights of those 2,500 serials which have begun publication since January 1, 1986, and for new subject headings, such as animal welfare, men's health, women's health, and New Age publications.

Gale Directory of Publications. This directory is an annual guide to newspapers, magazines, journals, and related publications. This directory is organized into sections by states and Canadian provinces and includes cross-reference sections by topics (alphabetically), newspaper feature editors (name, address, phone), and special topics, including agricultural college, foreign language, religious, trade and technical, fraternal, general circulation, and black publications, as well as newsletters and magazines.

Daily newspapers and daily periodicals, as well as weekly, semi-weekly, tri-weekly, and free circulation newspapers, are also cross-referenced into sections. There is also an alphabetical index by name and phone number of every publication listed in this directory.

To qualify for listing in *Gale Directory of Publications*, publishers must meet several criteria, including the following: (1) point of origin must be either the United States, Puerto Rico, or Canada; (2) frequency of publication—all publications may qualify; however, as a general policy, publications of primary and secondary schools, houses of worship, and internal "house organizations" publications are excluded; (3) source materials— usually the publisher, and occasionally the editor, president, or general manager, is the source contacted for candidate materials; (4) subjective value judgment is applied to the previous three criteria.

Computer-Based Indexes

INFOTRAC. This resource is issued monthly and contains two services searched separately. The Expanded Academic Index covers over four hundred periodicals of general and scholarly interest as well as *The New York Times*. The social sciences, humanities, economics, current affairs, science, and technology are covered. On-line access corresponds in part to ACADEMIC INDEX 1976–Present, issued monthly; MAGAZINE INDEX, and MAGAZINE ASAP 1959-3/1970; from 1973 to present is issued weekly.

PsycLIT. Another resource is *PsycLIT*, which is issued quarterly and provides indexes and abstracts in the fields of psychology and the behavioral sciences. Abstracts and indexes correspond to Psychological Abstracts. It covers international psychology literature and related fields of education, business, medicine, and law and includes access to over thirteen hundred journals as well as conferences, books, and dissertations. On-line access can be achieved by inserting PsychINFO into a system tied to a data base that supports these indexes.

MATHSCI DISC. MATHSCI DISC is updated twice a year and includes mathematics and computer science research literature. Citations appear with extensive reviews corresponding to Mathematical Reviews, Current Mathematical Publications, and Current Index to Statistics. The international literature of mathematics is covered, with heavy emphasis on original Russian journals; included are sixty journals translated from Russian and Chinese journals. Most reviews are in English. In addition to some sixteen hundred journals, coverage includes books and conference proceedings. Subfiles include ACM Guide to Computing Literature, 1984–Present; Computing Reviews, 1984–Present; Technical Reports in Computer Science, 1954–Present; and Index to Statistics and Probability, 1910–1968. On-line access may be achieved by inserting *MATHSCI*. It is issued on a monthly basis from 1973.

Current Contents on Diskette. Current Contents on Diskette (CCOD) is a weekly reader updating service. The index is set up in author, author location, title word(s), journal title, and subject listings corresponding to recently published periodical articles and selected new book chapters. It is available in five sections, each searched separately and one week at a time. A search profile can be stored and rerun automatically for each week. Subject areas include agriculture, biology and earth sciences; engineering, technology, and applied science; life sciences; physical, chemical, and earth sciences; and social and behavioral sciences. On-line access for the latest twelve monthly issues can be retrieved by typing *CURRENT CONTENTS SEARCH* (for searching all sections together); sections can also be searched separately on-line via the various CCON data bases.

Abstract Journal in Earthquake Engineering. Abstract Journal in Earthquake Engineering (AJEE) is a series of volumes published by the National Information Service for Earthquake Engineering—Earthquake Engineering Research Center at the University of California at Berkeley. AJEE is a comprehensive collection of abstracts and citations of world literature relevant to earthquake engineering and hazards mitigation. I looked at volume 15 when developing this part of the book and found that it included abstracts of technical papers, research reports, books, codes, and conference proceedings drawn from 141 technical journals and publications of academic, professional, and governmental organizations in twenty-four countries. A section of the volume also lists the specific journals surveyed, with addresses. It also contains the section Suggestions for Contributors, which provides specific information for a writer who wishes to submit a paper to the compendium.

This kind of compendium is published in a number of fields. Investigate your discipline to determine where such sources exist. Record the correct volume, obtain published papers, review them, and become knowledgeable about the styles and topics accepted.

Available On-Line Data Base Services

Several commercial data bases are available for research purposes. Some of these are actually available "on-line" through the use of a telephone line and personal computer, making it possible for the writer to work from an office or home.

One very popular on-line data base is *DIALOG* Information Services, Inc. *DIALOG* covers most subject areas. It contains over 400 on-line data bases in the sciences, technology, business, news, humanities, and the arts. It can be accessed by either modem or CD-ROM. Table 3-2 presents some of the data bases available through *DIALOG*.

Another resource worth becoming familiar with is the *Online Computer Library Center*, also known as *OCLC*. Formerly used primarily by librarians

Table 3-2
Data Bases Available through DIALOG

Topic	Data Base	Topic	Data Base
Agriculture/Food Science	AGRICOLA (U.S. National Agricultural Library)	Energy/Environment	APTIC (Air Pollution)
	COMMONWEALTH AGRICULTURAL BUREAUX ABSTRACTS		ENERGYLINE
	CRIS (Current Agricultural Research)		ENVIROLINE
	FOODS ADLIBRA		ENERGY INFORMATION
	FOOD SCIENCE & TECHNOLOGY ABSTRACTS		ENVIRONMENTAL PERIODICALS BIBLIOGRAPHY
Business/Economics	ABI/INFORM (Management)		POLLUTION ABSTRACTS
	CEMINCAL INDUSTRY NOTES	Government Publications	AMERICAN STATISTICS INDEX
	DISCLOSURE		CONGRESSIONAL INFORMATION SERVICE INDEX
	ECONOMICS ABSTRACTS INT'L		GPO MONTHLY CATALOG
	EIS INDUSTRIAL PLANTS		NATIONAL TECHNICAL INFORMATION SERVICE
	EIS NON-MANUFACTURING ESTABLISHMENTS		PUBLIC AFFAIRS INFROAMTION SERVICE
	FOREIGN TRADERS INDEX		PTS FEDERAL INDEX
	MANAGEMENT CONTENTS	Humanities/Arts	AMERICA: HISTORY & LIFE
	PHARMACEUTICAL NEWS INDEX		ART BIBLIOGRAPHIES MODERN
	THE PREDICASTS GROUP		HISTORICAL ABSTRACTS
	TRADE OPPORTUNITIES		LANGUAGE & LANGUAGE BEHAVIOR ABSTRACTS
	U.S. EXPORTS		MLA BIBLIOGRAPHY (Language & Lit)
Contracts/grants/current research	CRIS (Current Agricultural Research)		PHILOSOPHER'S INDEX
	FOUNDATION DIRECTORY		RILM ABSTRACTS (Music)
	FOUNDATION GRANTS INDEX	Law/Current Topics	CONGRESSIONAL INFORMATION SERVICE INDEX
	FROST & SULLIVAN DM		LEGAL RESOURCE INDEX
	GRANTS DATABASE		MAGAZINE INDEX
	GPO MONTHLY CATALOG (Gov't Pubs)		NATIONAL NEWSPAPER INDEX
	NATIONAL FOUNDATIONS		NCJRS (Criminal Justice)
	SSIE CURRENT RESEARCH		NEWSEARCH
Medicine	BIOSIS PREVIEWS		PAIS (Public Affairs)
	EXCERPTA MEDICA		PTS FEDERAL INDEX
	INTERNATIONAL PHARMACEUTICAL ABSTRACTS	Non Bibliographical	BIOGRAPHY MASTER INDEX
	IRL LIFE SCIENCES		CHEMNAME
	NIMH (Mental Health)		CHEMSEARCH
	PSYCHOLOGICAL ABSTRACTS		DISCLOSURE
	SCISEARCH		EIS INDUSTRIAL PLANTS
			EIS NON-MANUFACTURING ESTABLISHMENTS

Science

AQUACULTURE
AQUALINE
AQUATIC SCIENCES & FISHERIES ABSTRACTS
BIOSIS PREVIEWS (Life Sciences)
CHEMICAL ABSTRACTS GROUP
CA SEARCH
CHEMNAME
CHEMSEARCH
CHEMSIS
CONFERENCE PAPERS INDEX
DISSERTATION ABSTRACTS
GEOARCHIVE
GEOREF
INSPEC (Physics)
IRL LIFE SCIENCES
INTERNATIONAL PHARMACEUTICAL ABSTRACTS
OCEANIC ABSTRACTS
SCISEARCH
SPIN (Physics)
TSCA INITIAL INVENTORY (Chemical Substances)

Technological/Engineering

BHRA FLUID ENGINEERING
CLAIMS/CHEM (Chemical Patents)
CLAIMS/CHEM/UNITERM (Patents)
CLAIMS/CLASS (Patent Classification)
CLAIMS/U.S. PATENT ABSTRACTS
COMPENDEX (Engineering Index)
INPADOC (Patents)
INSPEC (Computers, Electronics)
ISMEC (Mechanical Engineering)
METADEX (Metals)
NATIONAL TECHNICAL INFORMATION SERVICE
NON-FERROUS METALS ABSTRACTS
PIRA (Paper, Printing, Packaging)
RAPRA (Rubber & Plastics)
SURFACE COATINGS ABSTRACTS
TRIS (Transportation)
WELDASEARCH
WORLD ALUMINUM ABSTRACTS
WORLD TEXTILE ABSTRACTS

Social Sciences

ENCYCLOPEDIA OF ASSOCIATIONS
FOREIGN TRADERS INDEX
FOUNDATION DIRECTORY
FROST & SULLIVAN DM
NATIONAL FOUNDATIONS
NICEM
NIMIS
PTS INTERNATIONAL TIME SERIES
PTS U.S. TIME SERIES
TRADE OPPORTUNITIES
TSCA INITIAL INVENTORY
U.S. EXPORTS
U.S. PUBLIC SCHOOL DIRECTORY
AIM/ARM (Vocational Education)
AMERICAN STATISTICS INDEX
CHILD ABUSE & NEGLECT
DISSERTATION ABSTRACTS
ERIC (Educational Research)
EXCEPTIONAL CHILD EDUCATION RESOURCES
LIBRARY & INFORMATION SCIENCE ABSTRACTS
NCJRS (Criminal Justice)
NICEM (Educational Media)
NIMIS (Media for Handicapped)
POPULATION BIBLIOGRAPHY
PSYCHOLOGICAL ABSTRACTS
SOCIAL SCISEARCH
SOCIOLOGICAL ABSTRACTS
U.S. POLITICAL SCIENCE DOCUMENTS
U.S. PUBLIC SCHOOL DIRECTORY

for cataloging books and arranging interlibrary loans, OCLC is becoming a widely used computerized bibliographic data base. This organization has activated a computerized system for reference searches called *FirstSearch*. It is user-friendly and aimed directly at library patrons such as academicians. *FirstSearch* allows scholars to tap into OCLC's bibliographic data base to search by keywords for journal articles, books, and other materials on a variety of subjects (see Table 3-3); a menu system makes this search capability possible. Users are able to order and obtain journal articles through the mail or over facsimile (FAX) machines.

Table 3-3
FirstSearch **Data Base**

Category	Data Base
BUSINESS/LAW	Business Periodicals Index Wilson Business Abstracts Index to Legal Periodicals
GENERAL/BOOKS/ SERIALS	OCLC Online Union Catalog Faxon's Periodical Delivery Service Readers' Guide to Periodical Literature Reader Guide Abstracts Library Literature Cumulative Book Index Book Review Digest
SCIENCE/TECHNOLOGY	Applied Science and Technology Index Biological and Agricultural Index General Science Index GeoRef BIOSIS Compendex
HUMANITIES/ART	Art Index Essay and General Literature Humanities Index
SOCIAL SCIENCE	PAIS (Public Affairs Information Service) Social Science Index
CONSUMER/PEOPLE	Consumers Index to Product Evaluations and Information Sources Matter of Fact Biography Index
EDUCATION	ERIC (Educational Resources Information Center) Education Index

OCLC's primary data base is the *Online Union Catalog*. Presently the *Catalog* contains nearly 25 million bibliographic records. The data base contains information about books, periodicals, audio recordings, musical scores, audiovisual media, maps, archives and manuscripts, and computer files.

OCLC also has a reference system called the EPIC Service, which allows librarians to perform searches for faculty by browsing through lists of books and other materials that are in the *Online Union Catalog*. It permits librarians to search within seven other data bases, such as the Consumers Index to Product Evaluations and Information Sources.

In addition to the seven data bases now carried on EPIC, OCLC has contracted with several additional vendors to provide access to more data bases.

Until the development of data bases such as *FirstSearch* and EPIC, scholarly research was largely a tedious trek through card catalogs or immense bibliographies. *FirstSearch* users will now be able to receive a copy of a journal (over ten thousand journals will be available) via standard delivery services, overnight mail, or facsimile machines. Table 3-4 presents typical on-line reference sources available through these various sources.

General and Specialized Directories

Scholars may also find the following publications very useful.

GPO Monthly Catalog. The U.S. government has a stockpile of useful data. Consider looking at the *GPO Monthly Catalog*. This data base contains references and an index to government publications corresponding to the printed copy of the *Monthly Catalog of United States Government Publications*. In addition, many federal publications are currently being made available via CD-ROM.

Books in Print Series. Books in Print is an annual publication produced from a data base of bibliographic publications. The data base includes scholarly, popular, adult, juvenile, reprint, and other types of books covering all subjects. Bibliographic entries contain author, co-authors, editors, co-editors, translator, title, original title, number of volumes, volume number, edition, whether reprinted, Library of Congress catalog number, subject information, series information, language other than English, whether illustrated, page numbers, ISBN, imprint, publisher, and distributor. This publication contains all in-print and forthcoming titles for more than thirty-three thousand publishers.

Several related series are always available to the researcher.

Subject Guide to Books in Print, which is published annually, lists all in-print and forthcoming titles except fiction, literature, poetry, and drama by one author, under more than sixty-six thousand Library of Congress subject headings.

Table 3-4
Typical CD-ROM: Computer-Assisted Information Services

Category	Data Base	Coverages	Periodically Updated
Business	ABI/INFORM	-business & industry international; -administration & management;	monthly
	DISCLOSURE	-US business & industry directory -corporate finances -US securities	monthly
	Dow Jones News/ Retrieval Service	-company news -press releases	daily
	EconLIT	-index to international literature -corresponding to the <u>Journal of</u> <u>Economic Literature</u>	quarterly
	Government Publications, US	-federal publications of major reference value	------
	GPO Monthly Catalog	-index to US government publications -corresponding to Monthly Catalog of US Government Publications	bi-monthly
	Index to United Nations Documents and Publications	-index to documents, official records, periodicals and sales publications of UN General Assembly	quarterly
	National Trade Data Bank	-full text international economics data	monthly
	NEWSBANK	-index to selected newspaper articles	------
	PAIS	-public affairs, administration & policy, economics, social sciences	quarterly
	Price Waterhouse Research	-accounting and auditing literature	quarterly
General Reference	Dissertation Abstracts	-abstracts & index to Doctoral & Masters Theses corresponding to Dissertation <u>Abstracts International</u>	monthly

	ERIC	-abstracts & index to education literature -corresponding to <u>Current Index to Journals on Education</u>	montly
	MLA International Bibliography	-literature; linguistics; folklore references & index on subjects of linguistics, general literature & related subjects	quarterly
	New Grolier Electronic Encyclopedia	-corresponds to 1990 edition of Academic American Encyclopedia	------
	Sport DISCUS	-corresponds to <u>Sport Bibliography</u> -covers all aspects of sports	monthly
	Oxford English Dictionary	-full text -access to 12 volume dictionary	------
Humanities	Humanities Index	-arts & humanities -articles and books corresponding to <u>Humanities Index</u>	quarterly
Sciences & Health	Applied Science & Technology Index	-index to over 135 periodicals in science & technology	quarterly
	AGRICOLA	-index to agriculture, food & nutrition life sciences -corresponding to <u>Bibliography of Agriculture</u>	quarterly
	CLIMATEDATA	-historical climatalogical data for US & Canada	annual
	Hazardous Materials Information System	-directory type data on health, safety, packaging and disposal of hazardous materials	------
	MATHSCI DISC	-citations with extensive reviews -corresponding to <u>Mathematical Reviews</u> -math research literature -computer science literature	twice yearly
	MEDLINE	-medical, biomedical, allied health literature; corresponding to <u>Index Medicus</u>	monthly
	Pan American Health Organization	-five divisions of information including international health data, sanitary engineering, legislation, software & health policy	------

Table 3-4 (continued)

Category	Data Base	Coverages	Periodically Updated
Sciences & Health (Cont)	Science Citation Index	-corresponds to Science Citation Index -4500 scientific and technical periodicals	weekly
	Toxic Release Inventory	-data on industrial firms, 320 chemicals and 17,500 facilities	
Social Sciences	PsycLIT	-abstracts and index corresponding to Psychological Abstracts -over 1300 journals and conferences, books, and dissertations covered	quarterly
	Social Sciences Citation Index on CD	-index to 1400 journals in the social sciences and 4500 journals in the fields of natural, physical and biomedical sciences	quarterly
	SOCIOFILE	-abstracts & index corresponding to Sociological Abstracts -indexes over 1600 journals & monographs & conference proceedings	4 months
	ELECTROMAP	-general reference information for the world -State Department data, economic, general geographic information	------
	GEOINDEX	-geological maps published by the U.S. Geological Survey	
	GEOREF	-index by author and subject to the geological & geophysical literature of North America 1975 -- and the world from 1933 -corresponding to the Bibliography of North America Geology	quarterly
	Current Contents on Diskette	-index by author, title words, journal title, and subject corresponding to Social & Behavioral Sciences	weekly
	Enviro/Energyline Abstracts	-3 data bases with abstracts -environment abstracts -acid rain abstracts -energy information abstracts	weekly
	INFOTRAC	-400 periodicals of general and scholarly interest in the social sciences, economics, current affairs, science and technology, and humanities	weekly

Books in Series in the United States is a publication listing in-print and out-of-print titles in popular, scholarly, and professional series. Some professors have found a title in or related to their discipline for which they acquired copyright permission to research and update and then republished the updated version.

Children's Books in Print is an annual listing of all books for children. Grade or reading level, where available, is listed.

Scientific and Technical Books and Serials in Print contains an annual selection of entries on science and technology and includes a selection of the subject areas derived from the International Serials Data Base.

Medical and Health Care Books and Serials in Print is an annual listing, including entries on medicine, psychiatry, dentistry, nursing, and allied areas of health, and related serials listings.

Religious and Inspirational Books and Serials in Print is an annual listing, including entries on the world's religions and on allied religious and moral topics and related serials.

Related data bases include the following:

On Cassette, an annual bibliography of Spoken Word Audio Cassettes concerning subjects from well known books to radio shows, describing titles, authors, readers-performers, release dates, number of cassettes, running time, order numbers, ISBN numbers, producer-distributors, with a brief annotation.

Bowker's Complete Video Directory is a two-volume annual bibliography with video titles ranging from feature films to children's videos. How-to tapes to documentaries, sports to travel, listing much the same information as the *On Cassette* volume, are available for review.

Software Encyclopedia is an annual two-volume publication listing all available software for microcomputers. Full versions of each entry are given in the title index. Additional information consists of compatibility, memory required, customer support, ISBN, and bibliography.

A textbook data base also supports the following publications:

EL-HI Textbooks and Serials in Print contains a listing of in-print and forthcoming titles.

Forthcoming Books is a cumulative list of books published since summer and books to come through December.

Another good resource is the following:

Publishing, Distribution and Wholesalers of the United States contains the full company name and address for over fifty-two thousand publishers active in the United States. ISBN prefixes are also listed. It is useful when you are looking for suitable publishers and publisher sources.

Other Commercial Publications. The *Literary Market Place* provides information about publishers and the specific markets and topics in which they specialize, together with addresses. *Gale Directory of Publications and*

Broadcast Media is a similar directory of publishers, markets, and addresses, which also includes broadcast media sources.

Other Specialized Sources of Published Data. The federal government and other sponsoring organizations periodically publish useful material. For instance, the National Library of Medicare publishes an *AIDS Bibliography*, which contains AIDS-related publication information. You may find recent books and articles dealing with pre-clinical, clinical, epidemiologic, diagnostic, and prevention issues. It also contains references to works dealing with ethical concerns, educational strategies, public health administration, and other related topics.

Theses and Dissertations. Libraries hold theses and dissertations prepared by their university's graduate students. University librarians can borrow these documents from other collegiate library collectors. A publication which is useful for identifying pertinent theses and dissertations is *Dissertation Abstracts International* (DAI). DAI is a reference tool that provides monthly compilations of abstracts of doctoral dissertations. DAI compiles this information into the broad categories of sciences, humanities, and engineering abstracts, by key-word title index and author index.

Dissertation Abstracts Ondisc includes doctoral dissertations from 1861 and master's theses from 1962. Abstracts and an index to these documents correspond to Dissertation Abstracts International, Comprehensive Dissertation Index, American Doctoral Dissertations, and Masters Abstracts. Abstracts are included from 1980 for dissertations and from 1988 for master's theses; abstracts for earlier citations can be obtained from print sources. Coverage includes over five hundred universities throughout the world with a major concentration on North American institutions. To obtain on-line access key *DISSERTATION ABSTRACTS* and one file will appear.

FINALLY, DEVELOPING A MANUSCRIPT FOR PUBLICATION

The following chapters address the specifics of publication in various media. It is worth repeating that once a topic is chosen for scholarly writing, a writer needs to review the specific periodical, determine its style requirements (including bibliographic citation format) and prepare a manuscript accordingly. Likewise, scholarly books, conference papers, and commercial book proposals all have certain protocols which must be addressed. Each chapter addresses a specific medium.

REFERENCES

Applied science & technology index (1990). New York, H. W. Wilson.
Article clearinghouse catalog. (1989). Ann Arbor, MI: University Microfilms International.

Books in print. Titles A-F, 4. (1990–1991). New York: R. R. Bowker.

Books in series in the U.S., 4th edition. (1985). New York: R. R. Bowker.

Bowker's complete video directory. (1992). New York: R. R. Bowker.

Business Periodicals Index. (1990). December, *33*(4).

The Chicago manual of style, 13th edition, (1982). Chicago, IL: The University of Chicago Press.

Children's books in print. (1991–1992). New York: R. R. Bowker.

DIALOG information retrieval service directory. (1983). Palo Alto, CA: Lockheed Missiles & Space Company.

Education Index. (1990). December, *62*(4).

EL-HI textbooks and serials in print. (1991). New York: R. R. Bowker.

Encyclopedia of associations, 25th edition. (1991). Princeton, NJ: Gale Research.

Forthcoming Books. (1991). August, *26*(4).

Henson, K. T. (1987). *Writing for professional publication.* Bloomington, IN: Phi Delta Kappa Educational Foundation.

Koek, K. E., & Winklepleck, J. (editors). (1991). *Gale directory of publications and broadcast media: An annual guide to publications and broadcasting stations.* Detroit: Gale Research.

Literary market place: The directory of the American book publishing industry. (1991). New York: R. R. Bowker.

Market A., & Rinn, R. C. *Author's guide to journals in psychology, psychiatry, and social work.* New York: Haworth.

Medical and health care books and serials in print. (1991). New York: R. R. Bowker.

National Information Service for Earthquake Engineering. (1990). *Abstract Journal in Earthquake Engineering,* Earthquake Engineering Research Center, April 15(2).

Neff, G. T. (editor) (1990). *1990 writer's market: Where & how to sell what you write.* Cincinnati: Writer's Digest Books.

1987 Gale directory of publications, 119th edition. (1987). Princeton, NJ: Gale Research.

On Cassette. (1992). New York: R. R. Bowker.

Publishing, distribution and wholesalers of the United States. New York: R. R. Bowker.

Religious and inspirational books and serials in print. (1987). New York: R. R. Bowker.

Scientific and technical books and serials in print. (1992). New York: R. R. Bowker.

Serials in print. New York: R. R. Bowker.

Social Sciences Index. (1990). December *17*(4).

Software encyclopedia. (1991). New York: R. R. Bowker.

Subject guide to books in print. (1991–1992). New York: Author. R. R. Bowker.

Subject guide to books in print. (1990). New York: R. R. Bowker.

Tennant-Neff, G. (editor). (1987). *The writers essential desk reference.* Cincinnati, OH: Writers Digest Books.

Thomas, R. C., & Ruffner, J. A. (1982). *Research centers directory,* 7th edition, Detroit: Gale Research.

Ulrich's International Periodicals Directory, 27th edition. (1988–1989). New York: R. R. Bowker.

U.S. Department of Commerce, National Technical Information Service (1990). *FEDIX: An on-line information service for universities and other research organizations: User's guide.* Washington, DC: U.S. Department of Commerce.

U.S. Department of Education, Office of Educational Research and Improvement (1986). *Directory of ERIC information service providers*. Washington, DC: U.S. Department of Education.

U.S. Department of Health and Human Services, K. Patrias (editor). (1987). *AIDS Bibliography, 1986–1987*. Washington, DC: National Library of Medicine.

U.S. Federal Emergency Management Agency. (1987). *Learning resource center user's guide*. Emittsburg, MD; U.S. Federal Emergency Management Agency.

U.S. Government Printing Office. *GPO style manual*. Washington, DC: U.S. Government Printing Office.

Van Leunen, M. (1992). *A handbook for scholars*. New York; Oxford University Press.

Wilson, D. L. (1991). New electronic journal to focus on research on medical treatments. *The Chronicle of Higher Education*, October 2, 38(7), A-27.

Wilson, D. L. (1991). Researchers get direct access to huge data base. *The Chronicle of Higher Education*, October 2, 38(7), A24-29.

Chapter 4

Writing for Professional Journals

REFEREED VERSUS NON-REFEREED JOURNALS

Henson (1987) discusses the viability of publishing in non-refereed journals—those journals which do not have an independent committee of experts or an editorial board to judge a manuscript's merits. Generally, university tenure and promotion committees and administrators prefer publication in refereed journals. These journals have an authoritativeness not often ascribed to their non-refereed counterparts. Yet, the distinction is not all that clear. Some editors of non-refereed journals use external consultants to assist in making publishing decisions—in a sense as referees. And some editors of refereed journals do an initial screening of manuscripts and pre-judge putatively inappropriate manuscripts before reviewers can judge them. Many editors actually make the final decision, of course, only after considering referee judgments.

Factors to Consider

Factors to consider when deciding where to submit a manuscript are of three types: (1) the manner in which the manuscript will be reviewed and judged for publication (refereed versus non-refereed); (2) the writer's personal time frame requirements, based on the need to get into print; and (3) the intended audience.

Factors considered important by deans in weighing the value and scholarship of a journal article are important to understand when making decisions about where to submit manuscripts. Euster and Weinbach (1986) surveyed deans' quality assessment of faculty publications for tenure/promotion decisions. Table 4-1 presents their survey findings. While some of these factors are beyond our control (e.g., frequency of article's citations elsewhere), many can be useful indicators for planning a writing project.

To get into print quickly, and perhaps with material such as research notes or opinion pieces which might not be ideally suited for a data-based and/or a nationally recognized journal in the field, a lesser known (new or up-and-coming journal) or a local or state association or group-sponsored journal might be a wise choice. Quite simply, the competition is less stringent. However, the trade-off will be in the recognition of that publication at tenure/promotion time.

Knowledge of the readership will also help lead to an identification of the appropriate journal. Is the intended readership

- Colleagues in the field?
- Colleagues in allied or related fields?
- Practitioners such as schoolteachers?
- The general public?

If a goal is to write for a specific group (e.g., specific segments of practitioners; cross-disciplinary readerships) in order to share new knowledge with these bodies, it will then be necessary to identify their particular periodical medium. The trade-off here is that some of these are trade periodicals that often look for specific names who are recognized as experts in their fields. As such, these periodicals are usually not truly "refereed" journals. Publication in these journals, again, may not weigh as heavily as publication in a refereed journal.

What to Look for in a Journal

Table 4-2 presents an overview of some selected journals. It details information pertaining to the kind of readership; whether it is refereed in terms of a system described by Henson (1990); and the typical length of time it takes to go through the publication process.

Henson's three-point scale for rating a journal as refereed is used here (3 is the maximum rating). If the journal editor regularly sends the manuscript to a panel of referees for review and rating prior to making a publication decision, it receives 1 point. If this review is a blind review (i.e., the panel of reviewers do not know the manuscript's author), it receives an additional point. If the journal uses a standard rater evaluation form for the review process thus ensuring uniform manuscript evaluation, it receives an additional point. Academic writers are concerned about the referee style of a journal and need to be aware of its

Table 4-1
Deans' Evaluation of the Importance of Factors in the Quality of a Journal Publication

Possible Factor	Mean Assessment
1. Is the journal refereed?	3.66
2. Is the journal considered "major"?	3.36
3. Is the article full-length (vs "brief notes," etc.)?	3.23
4. Has the article frequently been cited in the literature?	2.98
5. What is the assessment of the article by colleagues outside the university?	2.89
6. Is the faculty member the primary author or a co-author?	2.78
7. What is the assessment of the article by colleagues within the university?	2.78
8. Has the article been reprinted elsewhere?	2.51
9. Is the article single-authored or multiple-authored?	2.47
10. Does the article reflect continuity of work in the area?	2.44
11. Did the faculty member pay for any publication costs?	2.14
12. Does the article have value for persons working in other disciplines?	2.12
13. Is the journal in social work or another field?	2.02
14. Is the article empirically-based or a "think piece"?	1.98
15. Was the article invited or contributed?	1.81

N = 78. 0 = little or no importance; 4 = very important.

review policies. Some journals print a policy statement; another option is to call the editor to inquire and request a written policy statement. It is, as noted before, important to understand what the journal's editorial board looks for when deciding upon an article to publish. Figure 4-1 depicts a typical call for manuscripts and a writer's information sheet for a refereed journal.

Many writers want to know the makeup of the editorial board. Are the names recognizable as key people in the field? Are research universities represented? (This often indicates a need for an empirical or qualitative research study kind of article.) Are industry-based people represented? A practical kind of article would be best suited for this type of audience.

Table 4-2
Journal Publication Particulars

Journal Title	Readership	Referee Category	Submission to Acknowledgement	Timelines to Decision	To Print
Journal of Staff, Program and Organization Development	community college educators	3	3 days	4 months	8 months
*Journal of Vocational Education Research	vocational/technical educators & researchers	3	35 days	3 months	14 months
Journal of Studies in Technical Careers	voc/tech educators/ comm college instructors	2	10 days	3 months	8 months
Journal of Ship Production	maritime engineers	3	6 days	2 months	3 months
Journal of Educational Technology Systems	instructional technologists	2	15 days	4 months	8 months
Journal of Industrial Teacher Education	industrial/technical teacher educators	3	3 months	8.5 months	13 months
*Journal of Instructional Development	instructional technologists	3	1 month	6 months	13 months
Journal of Vocational Special Needs Education	vocational educators special ed educators	3	8 days	4 months	10 months
Performance & Instruction	instructional technologists	2	1 month	5 months	6 months
Journal of Instructional Psychology	educational psychologists instructional technologists	3	35 days	2 months	4 months
Journal of Small Business Management	small business educators/researchers	3	40 days	6 months	16 months
Logistics Spectrum	logisticians & planners in defense industry	2	5 months	11 months	20 months
Business Journal	business researchers	3	80 days	10 months	21 months
Educational and Psychological Measurement	educational psychologists	3	10 days	6 months	20 months
Educational Evaluation and Policy Analysis	evaluation researchers	3	35 days	3 months	5 months
Community/Junior College Quarterly	community college educators/researchers	3	12 days	2 months	12 months
Evaluation & Program Planning	evaluation researchers	3	6 months	9 months	29 months

Figure 4-1
A Typical Call for Manuscripts and a Writer's Information Sheet for a Refereed Journal

Information for Authors

The *Journal of Industrial Teacher Education* is issued four times annually by the National Association of Industrial and Technical Teacher Educators. Published manuscripts are high-quality guest articles, refereed articles, "At Issue" essays, "Comments," reviews of books/media and computer hardware and software in an "Under Review" section, and special feature issues that report scholarly inquiry and commentary broadly related to industrial and technical teacher education, military training, and industrial training. A "Journal Feedback" section also reports results of evaluations of the *Journal*.

Submission Requirements
All manuscripts submitted for publication must be accompanied by a cover letter that specifies the section of the *Journal* for which the manuscript is intended and an abstract that describes the essence of the manuscript in 150 words or less. Manuscripts must conform to guidelines provided in the *Publication Manual of the American Psychological Association* (1983, third edition). Figures and line drawings must be submitted in camera-ready form.

Manuscripts should be submitted on a *microcomputer diskette* and in *letter-quality hard copy form*. The preferred format is IBM or IBM compatible personal computer using WordPerfect as the word processing program. Other acceptable programs include Microsoft Word, Multimate, Displaywrite 3, PFS Writes, Wang PC, Samna, WordStar, Volkswriter, and WordMarc. *The name of the word processing program used must be indicated in the cover letter*.

The first seven letters of the author's last name are used to name a diskette file. In coauthored or multiauthored articles, the first initial of each author's last name is used. For example, an article written by Smith, Smythe, and Schmidt would be named "SSS." The suffix reflects the date (month and day) of correspondence: An article written by Smith, Smythe, and Schmidt that was submitted to the Journal on June 20, 1989, would be named "SSS.620." Use the letters A, B, and C, however, instead of figures to represent the months of October, November, and December. In the example above, if the article were submitted on *November 20*, 1989, it would be named "SSS.B20."

The submission procedures are intended to facilitate editing and producing the *Journal*. They should not be interpreted as precluding authors without microcomputer capabilities from submitting manuscripts for publication consideration. Authors unable to meet word processing specifications are to contact the Editor.

From the *Journal of Industrial Teacher Education*. Vol. 29. Reproduced by permission of National Association of Industrial and Technical Teacher Educators, Columbus, Ohio, 1992.

Sometimes talking to others who have published in the journal in order to learn of the journal's practices and peculiarities can be useful.

Some journals charge for publication of papers; some require membership in their association or society. This raises a philosophical question: Do you wish to submit a manuscript which will require a submission fee? Consider the journal's position with regard to the last point. Journals are usually either association- or university-based and -sponsored receiving little financial support. Costs are relentless. A professional journal requires a source of adequate support and income; hence the fee protocol.

Some journals have also adopted various additional requirements for manuscripts accepted for publication. They range from page costs for printing to graphics costs for special graphics or photographs, in addition to association or society membership fees as a condition for publication of an article. It is useful to know these requirements when deciding upon a journal for which to submit a manuscript.

Submission time lines for manuscript review are also good to know. Journals usually have a rolling review policy: Manuscripts are reviewed as they are received. Some journals subscribe to themes (i.e., they group articles on like subjects) and put out calls for theme papers. More about this shortly.

It is probably best to review several editions of the journal and read the publisher's or editor's comments on the mission and goals of the journal. Become familiar with the kinds of articles published and with the writing style and tone. Some journals publish only empirical studies. Others are open to philosophical arguments, reviews of literature, case studies, and scientific inquiry. The following are mission statements of various journals:

The American Journal of Small Business
"To publish papers that significantly contribute to the advancement of knowledge in the field of small business."

Journal of Research in Education
"The mission of *The Journal of Research in Education* is to provide a forum for sharing scholarship among researchers and practitioners in education. Thus, the Editorial Board encourages submission of manuscripts that reflect the broad range of theoretical, empirical, and methodological interests and standards represented by the divisions of Eastern Educational Research Association. Most importantly, contributions should be original—new knowledge and insights to the field."

Journal of Vocational Education Research
"Publishes articles dealing with original research, research, research methodologies, reviews of research, and theoretical issues with implications for research. Manuscripts are selected for publication on the basis of significance to vocational education, scholarly style and quality, conclusions drawn and supported to disseminate knowledge about vocational education."

Another way to increase publication success rate is to identify the focus and themes of certain journals in a given field. Almost every journal runs theme editions periodically. These themes follow trends in a discipline. Gathering advance knowledge of the themes, target dates, format, writing style, and language used in a particular journal increases the likelihood of being published therein.

Likewise, some journals focus on specific lines of inquiry, philosophies, practices, and the like. Knowledge of these trends can either (1) increase chances for publications, if you subscribe to the same ideas; or (2) prevent you from wasting time if you do not, and thus limit the number of publication rejections you are likely to receive.

Kinds of Journal Articles

There are various kinds of journal articles: (1) reports of empirical research or qualitative studies, (2) review articles, and (3) philosophical arguments or theoretical articles. In each case the usual criteria used by peer reviewers for manuscript evaluation include (1) the article's significance to the field or discipline to which the journal is dedicated, (2) the comprehensiveness of the literature review, (3) the adequacy of attention given to the conceptual research methodology or framework, (4) the care in developing the research questions or hypotheses, (5) whether the research process adhered to rigorous standards, (6) care in drawing and supporting conclusions, (7) the organization of the manuscript and whether the stylistic guidelines of the manuscript were adhered to, and (8) the contribution made to the field of inquiry.

Empirical Study Articles. Empirical study articles are reports of original research. This research might be experimental, ethnographic, naturalistic, or qualitative in nature. Empirical study manuscripts consist of separate sections corresponding to the visual stages of the research process. These include (1) an introduction describing the development of the research problem and a statement of the purpose of the investigation, (2) a methodology section describing how the research was conducted, (3) a results section reporting the results that were found, and (4) a discussion section discussing and interpreting the data and describing the implications of these results to the discipline.

Review Articles. Review articles are critical evaluations (critiques) of the state of knowledge in a particular area of a discipline. The purpose of a review paper is to analyze previously published literature, putting it in a specific conceptual perspective. In such an article the writer organizes and synthesizes previously published work (other authors) in a given area. Alternatively one may evaluate a specific work or works, discussing a particular point of view in light of its strengths and weaknesses. Note, however, that a review is not an annotated bibliography. In a sense, it is calling attention to the current state of knowledge in a given field, in light of what has been done by others.

The success of a review article lies in its organization. A carefully prepared outline will help to develop the paper. It is important to sell a reader on the value of a review of literature article in the opening sentences; otherwise it will not be read. Literature review readers are quite diverse— they often include peers, other scholars in allied fields, and perhaps students. Reviews of literature are often used for teaching purposes. Consider the makeup of the audience when writing.

In a review article a writer often (1) defines and clarifies a problem; (2) summarizes previous investigations so as to inform others of the state of current research; (3) identifies relationships, contradictions, gaps, and inconsistencies in the literature; and (4) suggests the next step or steps in potentially solving a problem (*Publication Manual of the American Psychological Association*, 1989, p. 21). Review articles can be arranged by relationships of the parts to the whole. Conclusions are most important. Conclusions are derived from the analysis of the literature. A conceptual base helps to synthesize the literature and explain the findings. Bibliographic completeness in a review article is essential.

We regularly see "state-of-the-art" reviews which provide new insights and understanding in a field. In fast-moving technological areas, these reviews are very useful to scholars if they are prepared well.

There are numerous publications dedicated to reviews, often published annually, in specific fields. For instance, the "The Yearbook of Vocational Education" series published by the American Vocational Education Association targets specific topic areas each year.

It is helpful to speak with the editor of a targeted journal prior to submitting or even developing a review-type manuscript. Very often literature reviews are welcomed when done in a certain style or covering a specific topic.

Philosophical and/or Theoretical Articles. Philosophical and theoretical articles are presentations of a philosophical argument or theoretical model based upon analyses of literature in a given field. Unlike a review article, a theoretical article draws from the literature those constructs which support a theory which one desires to test, and perhaps apply. The writer analyzes the development of one or more existing theories in order to refine and develop its particular variables or constructs. One might only critically analyze an existing theory—or alternatively could propose a new theory or expound on a philosophical argument.

BASIC MANUSCRIPT PREPARATION GUIDELINES

Most journals require manuscripts to be prepared in accordance with a specific style guideline. One such guide is the *Style Manual of the American*

Psychological Association, third edition (1989). Another very popular style guide is the University of Chicago's *The Chicago Manual of Style*, thirteenth edition (University of Chicago Press, 1982).

The appearance or style of a manuscript conveys a first and very telling impression to its reader—the editor. First impressions *do count*. Noble (1989) surveyed twenty-three journal editors representing five countries to determine their opinions of what makes a manuscript immediately acceptable or unacceptable to editors.

Basic Stylistic Preparation

A manuscript with a professional appearance is an initial plus to editors. Noble found the following stylistic characteristics of immediate concern to an editor (in rank order):

1. Professional appearance
2. Author guidelines followed
3. Good writing clarity and style
4. Title of manuscript
5. High quality abstract

A practical point of importance—avoid submitting a manuscript for review which is printed on a dot-matrix printer. Dot-matrix print does not reproduce well, and the manuscript will be difficult to read. Many journals no longer accept dot-matrix manuscripts for review. A well printed and reproducible manuscript makes for a good start in the review process.

A first step is to review the policy guidelines of the journal and identify the required style. Determine the number of manuscript copies required by a journal. You should also be aware of photographic requirements for any visuals used (e.g, figures, charts, photos), journal charges to the author for printing of these special items, and graphics requirements for any graphs, slides, charts, and so on, before the manuscript production process and comply with them. It is wise to secure copyright release for any photographic items adopted or borrowed for the article well in advance, thereby preventing a later slowdown in the process.

Manuscript Layout

A scholarly manuscript usually has several parts: title and title page, abstract, introduction, method, results, discussion/conclusion, references, and appendix. The following guidelines and practical suggestions are offered to help produce a publishable manuscript.

Title and Title Page. Day (1988) offers some very realistic comments about article titles: "When an author prepares a title for his paper, he would do well to remember one salient fact: that the title will be read by thousands of people. Perhaps four people, if any, will read the entire paper, but many people will read the title" (p. 8). This is even more true today, given electronic abstracting and searching services. The title serves as a focal point for entering and cataloguing the paper into the data base. The ability for others to locate a writer's work will depend upon how it is described in the system.

Therefore, give considerable thought to a title. Make sure that it describes the dependent and independent variables and their relationships—all key elements of the work and study. The title should summarize the main idea of the work as simply as possible. Its principal function is to inform readers about the study.

Other parts of the title page in addition to the study title are the author's name(s) and affiliation(s). The author's name should be stated as first, middle, initial, and last name. Omit official titles. The affiliation identifies where the author(s) actually conducted the work or investigation. The author who was the primary principal investigator or made the major contribution should be listed first. Dual affiliations, as appropriate, can be used.

A running head is useful. The running head is an abbreviated title that is printed at the top of each page of the published article to identify the article for the reader. It should contain a maximum of fifty characters, including spaces. It is good practice to use a running head in any style used.

Abstract. An abstract enables a reader to identify the basic content of an article quickly. Euster and Weinbach (1986) document its importance to initial editor appeal. Its purpose is to permit the reader to determine whether the article is relevant to his or her needs without reading the entire article. Many journals require an abstract and set a limit of 150 words for it.

An abstract should contain principal objective(s) and scope of the work being described, methodology employed, summarized results, and primary conclusions. A note on conclusions—this is the single most important part of an article—they need to be stated in the abstract as well as in the introduction, and *in detail* in the discussion.

Day (1988) describes two kinds of abstracts: the informational abstract and the indicative abstract. Used principally by researchers to provide quick information about the content of an article to other researchers, the informational abstract is a short overview of the problem, method, principal data, and conclusions. The indicative (or descriptive) abstract is designed to indicate the content of the paper, much as a table of contents does, easing the reading task for potential readers. These are often used in review papers, conference reports, government reports, reports of literature, and the like. Figure 4-2 is a typical abstract of a naturalistic study report article.

Figure 4-2
A Typical Abstract of a Naturalistic Study Report Article

Evaluation and Program Planning, Vol. 14, pp. 113–122, 1991
Printed in the USA. All rights reserved.

A DISCREPANCY-BASED METHODOLOGY FOR NUCLEAR TRAINING PROGRAM EVALUATION

JEFFREY A. CANTOR

Lehman College, City University of New York

ABSTRACT

This paper describes a process for training program evaluation based upon Provus' Discrepancy Evaluation Model and the principles of instructional design. The Discrepancy-Based Methodology for Nuclear Training Program Evaluation was developed for use in nuclear power utility technician/operator training programs. It facilitates systematic and detailed analyses of multiple training program components in order to identify discrepancies between program specifications, actual outcomes, and industry guidelines for training program development. This evaluation is a three-phased process. Phase One analyzes utility program standards which define the program (what should be). Phase Two analyzes the programmatic data (what is). Phase Three synthesizes the multiple discrepancy analyses, culminating in interpretation and reporting of the evaluation findings.

Reprinted from *Evaluation and Program Planning* 14, Jeffrey A. Cantor, A discrepancy-based methodology for nuclear training program evaluation, pp. 113–122, copyright 1991, with permission from Pergamon Press, Headington Hill Hall, Oxford OX3 0BW, UK.

A good abstract is accurate—and contains no new information not cited in the actual paper. It is also self-contained, defining any specialized terminology, abbreviations, or acronyms. It should be concise, specific, and as brief as possible. It should report and not evaluate. Finally, it must be readable. This is often the only part of the article most people will read. It should *sell* the paper.

Introduction. Many writers of research articles begin writing the report while the research is in progress, as many of the elements of the process, as well as aspects of the methodology, are fresh in the writer's mind. The introduction of the paper is best written this way. An author begins by asking why he or she has assumed the particular line of inquiry.

A few introductory paragraphs are needed to introduce a reader to the rationale for selecting the problem area studied (why statement) and place the significance of the problem in the context of the field or discipline. No magic number of paragraphs must be included. Generally, the introductory paragraphs should develop the problem statement in two ways:

1. They introduce the reader to the problem. References from other experts/authorities in the field are absolutely appropriate here to validate

the points being made, often adding a dimension of significance to the research or scholarship reported.

2. They identify for the reader the need for the study or scholarship. This need may be a writer's perception but should also be related to the interests of the profession. It is appropriate to reference and document statements here, since a cumulative demonstration of need to study the problem area has more validity and "significance" than a writer's opinion. Figure 4-3 is a sample introductory paragraph.

Assume that readers have a general background in the field and do not need extensive reeducation. It is better to cite pertinent research and contributors and avoid non-essential detail. The probability that a reader will continue past the introduction rests on the ability to write an interesting and attention-catching introduction. It is important in the introduction, however, to describe the theoretical basis supporting the study or work briefly. Wherever possible, tie it to past work in an area. A successful writer demonstrates a knowledge of the field and past efforts in the area. Most reviewers look at this demonstration (or lack thereof) very carefully. If a writer fails to demonstrate this understanding and appears to solve a problem in a vacuum, a manuscript will not get very serious attention.

Purpose of the Study. Once the problem is introduced, if the article is a study, discuss the intended purpose (rationale) of conducting the work. Usually one or two paragraphs is sufficient to explain both the purpose and the problem statement. Here a writer tells the reader what the researcher proposes to do. The paragraph frequently begins, "The purpose of the research is to. . . ." It gives the problem statement in declarative form. The problem statement posed as a question is useful in planning the research, but more generally is stated as a declarative sentence in the research report. Figure 4-4 illustrates the way the purpose was stated in an article based on a case study.

Figure 4-3
A Sample Introductory Paragraph

INTRODUCTION

This paper describes a comprehensive process for commercial nuclear power training program evaluation. I initially developed this process for use at The Three Mile Island nuclear power facility to review and evaluate the training department and its training programs, which were redesigned to meet the facility's personnel training needs after the accident in 1979. Prior to the utility's start-up of the affected reactor, I was employed as a consultant to conduct a program evaluation of the critical technician/operator training programs (including licensed control room operator, chemical technician, etc.). That accident highlighted a need for rigorous review and evaluation of the utility's personnel training programs for licensed and nonlicensed control room operators and related critical operations technician training.

Figure 4-4
A Purpose of the Study Taken from an Article Based on a Case Study

Purpose of the Study

No resolution of this debate will be achieved in any ultimate sense. The varying circumstances of specific locales over time mean that in some cases collaborative efforts will be advantageous but in other cases may produce no discernible benefit. Nevertheless, new empirical information, derived by investigating specific examples in which collaboration has occurred, can improve our understanding of how communities coordinate job training and economic development efforts when such joint action is appropriate.

The purpose of the present study was to provide this new information. The study focused on identifying innovative job creation practices, including those involving (a) assistance to small business, a key ingredient in job creation and economic development for this country (Armington & Odle, 1982; Birch & MacCracken, 1982; U.S. Government Printing Office, 1983; U.S. Small Business Administration, 1985), and (b) benefits to JTPA participants or other low-income, hard-to-employ workers in terms of job placement. The study analytically assessed what works, why it works, and the lessons learned.

Once the purpose is established, state the hypothesis or research question(s) (experimental versus naturalistic design) and the methodology in general. This will provide clarity to the article. Specifically describe the variables that were manipulated, the results the researcher expected, and why. Figure 4-5 is the research hypothesis paragraph following the purpose section (see Figure 4-4) in the case-study report previously discussed.

Figure 4-5
A Research Hypothesis Paragraph

Research Hypotheses

Hypotheses were developed about why organizations collaborated and about the structure of interorganizational arrangements. The main hypothesis was that a single coordinating organization would be found at the hub of the interorganizational arrangement and that this organization would have been newly formed for the purpose of combining job training and economic development activities. A second hypothesis was that informal networks, for example, resulting from overlapping board memberships, were the more important ingredients in making arrangements work, compared with formal arrangements among organizations.

From Jeffrey A. Cantor. (1990). Job training and economic development initiatives: A study of potentially useful companions. *Educational Evaluation and Policy Analysis,* Summer 12[2], 121–138. Copyright (1990) by the American Educational Research Association. Reprinted by permission of the publisher.

The research design selected dictates whether this section is called "Subproblems" or "Research Questions." Usually the listing is not lengthy, possibly ranging from two to six enumerated questions.

Ensure that a clear statement is made to demonstrate continuity between previous and present work. APA and other style guides require that the problem be described clearly enough to ensure breadth and clarity—to make it understandable to a wide professional audience. Issues surrounded by controversy should be treated fairly.

Two additional kinds of information should now be presented, depending on the kind of study reported:

1. Delimitations/Limitations. Describe the way in which the research has been circumscribed, the sample used, the instrumentation used, and the way the data were collected. Often one may provide the rationale for any delimitation.

Once the data have been collected, analyzed, and interpreted, one may need to identify "limitations," such as uncontrollable difficulties which occurred during the study. For example, one researcher had been in the midst of collecting data from high school teachers in San Francisco on October 17, 1989; after the earthquake several schools were closed and teachers were shifted from one school to another. Researchers may have limitations which could not be planned for but affected data collection. Such difficulties must be reported in the article.

2. Definitions. It is helpful to define each word or word unit used that could be confusing to the reader or is being used in a special way. For example, senior high school may include grades 10 to 12 or grades 9 to 12. And the age level of students being studied may make a difference. Describe what is meant by senior high school in the context of the article. Also, ensure that any acronyms are clearly defined. For example, Lehman High School has a WOW program, probably referred to as "wow" by the teachers and staff at that school and no doubt understood by them. However, it would not be understood elsewhere.

Review of the Literature. Two major purposes are served by the review of the related literature presented in this section of the manuscript: (1) the writer describes for the reader the extent of the literature and research in the field and the extent of the supporting search; (2) the writer identifies the existing knowledge about the topic/problem statement and shows how a void is to be filled by the research undertaken.

There are secondary purposes to the review of related literature, too. These may be satisfied by (1) opinions or perspectives about the problem area (usually generalized from recent opinion articles) and (2) findings of previous research studies which are supported or contrasted with the researcher's findings. The latter purpose is very important. The writer may have needed to use those findings as one presented the findings and made comparisons and contrasts.

A third purpose is clarification of its theoretical base on which one's study purpose and design rest. That base must be made absolutely clear to the reader. Consider some aspects of the research design: Is there a body of literature that needs to be discussed relating to the dependent variable(s)? How about the independent variable(s)? What about each sub-problem? What about the hypotheses? Each of these areas may provide a fruitful "topic" for clarifying the discussion. A separate section, often called the "theoretical or conceptual base," may be needed. This section is included to describe any theory developed by previous researchers which is used as the basis for the study design and analysis. For example, if a researcher were to tape record the language exchange of a business analysis class and analyze the kind of cognitive or thought processes which the teacher was eliciting from males versus females of fifteen-year-olds versus seventeen-year-olds, one might very well wish to describe and explain Arno Bellack's theory of the language of the classroom. This theory was based on Wittgenstein's games theory. The research reported is to be an extension of, and in part a replication of, a theory which has already been established.

Finally, the review of the related literature should not be a series of connected or disconnected annotations of each article. Rather, the information one wishes to convey to the reader is organized systematically and/or topically (perhaps by variable in an experimental study or concept in a naturalistic one). Figure 4-6 is a typical review of the literature establishing a conceptual framework for a naturalistic study.

Method. The method section presents an overview of how the research or project was conducted. It is intended to inform the reader of what was done and how. The reader (including the peer reviewer) will use this information to judge the appropriateness of the selected methodologies. Defend the methodology in this sub-section. Be aware of the need to comply with the ethical principles guiding the research organization. The reader will look for a match between research questions or hypotheses and methodology. It can also be used by other researchers to replicate the study. Certain information must be included, such as (1) subjects, including population/ sample; (2) materials/apparatus; and (3) procedures.

Population and Sample. The population and sample sub-section should describe the subjects who were the focus or who participated in the study, including how many participated and how they were selected and, depending on the study, the size of both the population and the sample. Sometimes it is necessary to defend decisions regarding sample size. Also, if a survey was conducted, defend the percentage of returns. If sampling procedures were used, describe sampling procedures and randomization. Defense of sample stratification is important, as in sample size.

The reader needs to know about the data which was collected to address the problem statement, including demographic data. Available sample descriptors should be written into this section. Figure 4-7 is a methodology section for a case study.

Materials and Apparatus. The materials and/or equipment used in the research should also be described. Depending on the kind of work done, this may be laboratory equipment, timekeeping devices, curriculum innovations, instructional technology, physical fitness devices, and so on. The procedures used to develop and/or acquire them are also important.

Procedures. Each step in the execution of the experimental design or in the research process of choice should be discussed and described. Where applicable, cite references to the methodological process adopted for the study. Use graphics as necessary. This section should tell the reader what was done and how. Sub-headings should set off each method sub-section.

For experimental or quasi-experimental studies: Here it is essential to describe the assignment of the treatment to the subjects, as well as the exact experimental procedures employed. Describe the selection or development of all treatment material (e.g., computer programs used for the experiment or criterion measures or instruments). Identify whether (and why) certain subjects were eliminated from the study. Describe what the test(s) consists of and why it contains those elements.

Figure 4-6
A Typical Review of the Literature Establishing a Conceptual Framework for a Naturalistic Study

THE MODEL - A CONCEPTUAL FRAMEWORK

The ultimate objective of training program evaluation in the nuclear power industry is to ensure that the program produces competent technician/operators capable of safe reactor operation. To meet this objective an evaluation process must: provide a means to systematically collect, review, and analyze critical employee (technician/operator) performance data; match the data against utility personnel procedures and engineering specifications against industry (INPO) and government (NRC) guidelines and policy; and, ultimately, match the data against operator performances and the utility's own overall performance record.

Nuclear Utility Training
Technicians need to be familiar with the overall control room function and be competent in their respective technical specialties. They need to be able to react instantly to emergency situations such as signals and indications. The instructor is the primary professional in nuclear power training. Thus, the following discussion concerning training program evaluation centers around the instructor, and is provided to highlight the training function in the utility and the manner in which training decisions are made using evaluation data from utility plant operations and technician performances.

The TMI training program is an integral part of the overall utility operation. All training staff including instructors are appointed from senior technical and engineering ranks within the utility. The training staff makes all decisions about what kinds of training will be provided. Training needs assessment data are continually collected to determine formal training requirements.

Data are collected (and computer archived) from incumbent technician/operators, engineering documents and requirements, and utility operating procedures to determine each required job/task function. For instance, if evidence exists that training is needed on the operation of a control valve, engineering specifications data are provided to the training department by an engineering operations technician. Together, the engineering technician and instructor analyze the data to determine the knowledge and performance requirements needed to operate the valve. This forms the basis for instruction on valve operation.

Feedback regarding technician/operator on-the-job performance problems is also obtained from personnel such as senior technicians and operators, utility operations managers, and technician supervisors. This occurs in regularly scheduled committee meetings composed of engineering, management, and training personnel. The training and development process also includes review of technician/operator performance records which are analyzed and compared to existing job performance requirements. At these meetings, problems related to technician errors on the job are surfaced for discussion with recommendations for training as necessary. Data are also obtained from the training program records concerning student (technician/operator) performance within formal courses.

Utility training is designed as a closed-loop process in which data derived from all of these sources form the input to a systematic procedure for both technician/operator and training program review and evaluation.

The Instructional Systems Design Process
It is important to understand that TMI utility technician/operator training is designed and developed by utility instructors using an instructional systems design approach (ISD) (Cantor, 1986a) and according to specific objectives which describe the responsibilities, personnel requirements, and training design requirements and methods. These ISD processes include a structure for training needs analysis, training program design, development, implementation, and evaluation. ISD is a logical systematic process for defining worker competency requirements, developing worker performance objectives, instructional delivery media, and training and trainee evaluation strategies (Fig. 1).

Within the nuclear power industry, ISD is detailed in an industry-promulgated standard for instructional development and training program operation which is endorsed and used by all licensed nuclear power utilities. The Institute for Nuclear Power Operation (INPO) maintains these industry-developed guidelines and procedures to complement the Nuclear Regulatory Commission's statutes and regulations. Included are specific performance requirements for the personnel who are responsible for the operation and maintenance of the reactor, control room, peripheral controls, and instrumentation. These ISD standards were used as a foundation for development of the comprehensive discrepancy-based evaluation process.

In the case of TMI, a multifaceted training evaluation was conducted. This process had to provide both formative evaluation findings for immediate program attention, and summative findings for periodic review and reporting to external governmental and policy-making organizations. Initially, the process needed to be implemented by my external review team for the accreditation visit, and later institutionalized into an on-going internal personnel evaluation process.

Figure 4-7
A Methodology Section for a Case Study

Methodology

The Case-Study Method

The case-study methodology was selected because it provides for systematically reviewing what is known regarding the factors influencing interorganizational collaboration and linkage, introducing new data and perspectives, and providing a structure for the development of policy recommendations. The concept of case enabled this researcher to define the boundaries of an investigation beyond those associated with a single data set or organization (Yin, 1989). As a research strategy, the distinguishing characteristic of the case study is that it attempts to examine (a) a contemporary phenomenon in its real-life context, especially when (b) the boundaries between phenomena and context are not clearly evident.

Replication design. The case-study methodology was enhanced through the use of a replication design, the aim of which is to demonstrate both "direct" and "systematic" replications (Yin, 1989). A direct replication occurs when similar phenomena lead to similar outcomes at two or more sites. The more frequently this pattern is observed - that is, the more replications there are - the more confidence can be placed in the findings. A systematic replication occurs when similar phenomena lead to similar outcomes at two or more sites. When this pattern occurs, the direct replications can then be interpreted as being applicable across these systematically varying characteristics, thereby increasing the generalizability of the findings.

Site Selection Process

Two criteria were used in selecting sites for analyses. First, a site had to show evidence of linking job training with economic development efforts, which produced sustained positive outcomes including (a) documentable job creation, (b) successful assistance to small businesses, and (c) a solid record placing JTPA-eligible persons in jobs. Second, a site had to include the joint actions of two or more service providers, in which either different organizations collaborated or a single organization linked the activities of different service providers. They also had to meet certain distributional criteria such as different regions of the country, urban-suburban-rural settings, ethnic or racial groups as target employment populations, and regional economies.

A broad array of 62 eligible sites was nominated, identified, and screened through a two-stage process. These nominated sites were contacted, and information was obtained regarding their characteristics. Of further interest were 22 sites that appeared to demonstrate the relevant range of programmatic activities (job training and economic development) and involved collaboration or partnership among two or more organizations.

A total of six sites were selected for study, permitting a minimal number within which two types of replications would be sought. The following sites were selected for case study:

- o Pima County Community Services Department - the JTPA operating agency (Tucson, Arizona)
- o Northeast Florida PIC, Inc. (Jacksonville, Florida)
- o Susquehanna Region PIC, Inc. (Havre de Grace, Maryland)
- o Chester County Partnership for Economic Development, Inc. (West Chester, Pennsylvania)
- o Greater Grand Rapids Economic Area Team (Grand Rapids, Michigan)
- o Seattle-King County Economic Development Council (Seattle, Washington)

For naturalistic (i.e., descriptive) studies: Defend the development of the data-gathering instrument(s). Provide a complete description of all respondents (the number of subjects or cases from which data gathering was attempted) and the number of usable and complete sets. The reader wants to know these percentages.

For all research: Describe the procedures used for the validation of the data-gathering instrument or criterion of measurement. Discuss briefly any pilot study procedures used, including difficulties encountered. The final words deal with procedures used to analyze the data. Identify here the tabulation procedures used, and any statistical procedures which were applied to the data gathered.

Results. Authors draw conclusions based on the analyses of the raw data. Initially, state the principal findings of the study. Provide sufficient detail in the data analysis to support the findings. Cite all relevant findings, especially those that run counter to the hypothesis. There are three parts of the results section: (1) description of results, (2) explanation of any seeming inconsistencies or discrepancies in the results, and (3) comparison of current findings with those in other studies. Figure 4-8 is a typical results section from a case study. The description, explanation, and comparison may not necessarily be in three separate sequential sections, rather, one may describe data for a question, item, and so forth, and note explanations of discrepancies and comparisons with other studies for each. Or it may be done in sections; no hard and fast rule exists. Just keep the reader in mind: how can one present the data in a way that will make sense to the reader? One final comment: Not all studies will have other comparable studies to use. A researcher who is truly breaking new ground cannot compare results with those of other studies.

In this section figures and tables clarify data presentation. Center text description to highlight the findings of the data analysis, not to repeat data already presented in tabular form. Be clear and specific about statistics presented. Include information about the obtained value of a test reported (i.e., degrees of freedom, probability level). Include descriptive statistics (means, standard deviations).

Tables. Tables help to reduce narrative. While the table shows the data (in readable, understandable, complete form), the narrative section for each table should point up any trends, contrasts, or seemingly inconsistent figures or data in the table. Narrative is also used to make comparisons among groups (e.g., males versus females, co-op versus non-co-op students). It is often helpful to point out degrees of differences (twice as many, for example) and to provide explanations for a logical finding— that is, a finding that makes sense to you, the expert. *Titling* of tables is extremely important. They should be presented and titled in such a manner that one need not read the text to understand them; they should be self-explanatory. The title should make completely clear what the table

Figure 4-8
A Typical Results Section from a Case Study

A Planning and Development Model

The national study (Yin, et. al., 1989) produced new information regarding the role of occupational education and community-technical colleges in the formation of linkages of occupational education (job training) and local economic development. The new information can be viewed and understood in a model for job training and economic development (Figure 4). This model describes the role of the community-technical college and other community-based interorganizational relationships in terms of: 1) organizational structures; 2) interorganizational memberships; 3) interorganizational operations; and 4) interorganizational activities. The model's dynamics involve a single organization at the center of an institutional arrangement responsible for both economic development and job training activities. However, contrary to our hypothesis, a new organization need not be created to support joint activities. This finding suggests that other locales may undertake joint job training and economic development efforts without necessarily creating a totally new organization to coordinate these activities. However, one single organization must assume a coordinating and leadership role. This organization can very well be a community-technical college.

Yin, et al. also noted that the process of economic development and job creation is often a prolonged activity; therefore an infrastructure capable of supporting and sustaining the process must be created or identified. Again, a community-technical college would be an appropriate resource.

Core Organizations in the Formal Arrangement

Tied to the target organization is always a small group of collaborating or core organizations. These support organizations include: a job training agency such as a community-technical college, community college, or a university; an economic development agency (whether part of the local government or not); and a chamber of commerce, as well as other governmental or quasi-governmental agencies. In some instances these organizations are private and/or nonprofit in nature. The composition of this group depends on the individual community and its goals.

The actions of these collaborating organizations are usually formally bound through contractual agreements, as hypothesized, or as a result of the legal arrangement itself (e.g., a partnership arrangement). The sites usually have contractual arrangements that exchange funding support for certain types of activities. Often as in the case of Harford Community College, a mission statement sets a tone or provides an impetus for action. Additional funding opportunities also materialize as a result of these linkages, such as through the JTPA, the Perkins legislation, etc. which serve as additional benefits from collaboration.

Community-technical colleges can bring these funding opportunities to the collaboration. In any event, a formal agreement is necessary to facilitate the collaborative effort.

Interorganizational Memberships

Representatives of these organizations often are part of boards of directors of other core organizations. Through both formal and informal associations, mutual exchanges of information and support occur. In fact, this finding alone proved to be the single most beneficial and catalytic resource leading to successful collaboration and linkage. Individual civic-minded personalities often contributed to the success of the whole in ways which were difficult to empirically document, but which were not definitely valid. Many long-range activities are sustained as a result of the drive and dedication of individuals in the collaboration. While these phenomena are critically important to the overall success of such collaborations, it is impossible to cause them to occur.

Interorganizational Operations

As stated in the study hypothesis, organizations link together when they can derive mutual beneficial exchanges from each other. Examples of mutual benefits derived from collaborative activities are the abilities to both conduct and sustain programs or projects over long periods of time; to be able to plan for extended activities; and to carry out long-range agendas. Community-technical colleges can access new sources of students, new employment opportunities for graduates, and varieties of resources through these collaborations. All of these activities are necessary for successful economic and manpower development. This finding can prove useful for justifying economic development mission statements for community-technical colleges, if similar mutually beneficial outcomes can be predicted from linkage arrangements.

Long-Term Benefits of Arrangements

Interorganizational arrangements likewise provide an important capability for dealing with economic development over an extended period of time. This capability is critical when planning strategies for developing job training programs within a college and a community. Interorganizational arrangements are desirable because they go beyond specific projects and programs to produce a longer-term capability in economic development. A locality can expect business expansion, job creation, and job training outcomes, possibly involving JTPA-eligible students from these joint efforts. The desired outcomes are two-fold: (1) that the economic development activity leads to the creation of new jobs; and (2) that the new jobs require, in part, the entry-level skills which are taught to the students in the program.

From Jeffrey A. Cantor. (1990). Occupational education, economic development and the role of the community college. *Journal of Studies in Technical Careers*, Fall xii(4), 323–326. Reproduced by permission of the Journal of Studies in Technical Careers, Carbondale, Illinois, 1992.

is about so that the reader need not refer to the text to know what the figures represent. The units should be clearly designated, whether they represent money, pupils, words per minute, or whatever. There are several guidelines concerning the use and notation of numbers. Any number that begins a sentence, title, or heading should be spelled out. As an example, MLA style spells numbers below 10 that do not represent precise measurements, but uses figures to express all numbers 10 and above. Figures should be used when numbers below 10 are compared with numbers 10 and above (for example, 3 of 14) and for all numbers that represent statistical or mathematical functions, times, dates, sample or population size, and scores. The reader should not have to read the explanations of the table in order to grasp the meaning of the numbers. Please refer to the appropriate manual (e.g., *APA, Chicago*) for a description of how tables are typed in its manuscript style.

Graphs. Comparisons, trends, or contrasts are more clearly illustrated by graphs than they are by tables of numbers. Polygrams (line graphs), histograms (bar charts), or pie charts are often used to depict comparisons, trends, or contrasts visually. When constructing the *polygram* or *histogram*, a good rule of thumb to keep in mind is the three-fourths rule: The vertical axis (ordinate) is normally three-fourths as long as the horizontal axis (abscissa). For comparison purposes (for example, males versus females), paired bars of different intensities (gray/black; solid/striped) may be used to provide a very effective picture of comparisons and contrasts. Use the proper scale and include a base line. Use the same sized interval for each unit of data, do not break the graph, and properly label the chart. Titling of charts is done in the same manner as titling of tables.

Discussion/Conclusion. Once the results have been presented, one is now in a position to evaluate and interpret the implications, as they apply to the research questions or hypotheses. In this section the writer is at liberty to examine and interpret and possibly qualify the findings. Draw inferences directly from the findings. Relate the findings to the theoretical framework. This section can be combined with the results section when the report is not too large. Figure 4-9 is a discussion/conclusions extract from a journal article.

There are some general guidelines for preparing a good discussion section. Begin with a clear statement of support or non-support for the original research questions. Then describe the findings as they relate to the original statements. First, present whatever relationships or generalizations are indicated by the results of the study. Discuss these findings, rather than restating them. Detail and highlight lack of correlation (i.e., exceptions) and state still unconfirmed points in the research. Discuss whether the findings and interpretations confirm or disagree with the literature review or other studies previously conducted. Some helpful points follow:

Figure 4-9
A Discussion/Conclusions Extract from a Journal Article

CONCLUSION

This article has discussed The Discrepancy-Based Methodology for Nuclear Training Program Evaluation developed for use in the nuclear power industry. This methodology was commissioned, financed, and designed to solve an immediate problem - the need for an empirical, multifaceted evaluation tool, capable of use in a complex, highly technical, and politically visible organization - a public utility. As a result of the design and development of The Discrepancy-Based Methodology for Nuclear Training Program Evaluation, a systematic methodology for identifying standards against which to assess program operation and successes, and a formative-summative discrepancy-based process to review ongoing programs was installed in the TMI utility. This methodology now offers the evaluation community at large a new and refreshing tool with which to make positive inroads in the world of large scale organizational evaluation as well as other multifaceted policy-setting environments. Further, this methodology allows an evaluator to gain a useful and unambiguous "big picture" in heretofore difficult kinds of organizational evaluations - including large and complex engineering organizations such as nuclear power, and so forth, and in climates affecting large budgets and socio-political constituencies.

Applicability to Policy Development
From a public policy perspective, The Discrepancy-Based Methodology for Nuclear Training Program Evaluation provides sound data for decision making affecting "big picture" critical issues such as nuclear power utility location, construction, organization, and licensing and regulation. This evaluation process has proven to provide a framework from which to use large-scale program evaluation data to make these "big picture" decisions about: the cost effectiveness of multi-million dollar programs; the overall manpower and budgetary needs of large-scale organizations, management and administrative competence; and, in the case of organizations such as nuclear power utilities, societal well-being and needs as well.

Within a power utility organization, decision making based on training program evaluation data includes indications for revisions in manpower planning and development activities including manpower logistics decision making relating to work crew planning, staffing, reorganizing, and so forth. Discrepancy-based evaluation provides program managers and policymakers an empirical basis for decision making about these critical employee performances.

Applicability to the Evaluation Discipline
I have found that all too often training program reviews amount to nothing more than cursory notations of individual perceptions and biases. However, as has been seen in the nuclear power-generating industry, significant policy decisions are based on the findings of substantive personnel

and training outcomes data. The Discrepancy-Based Methodology for Nuclear Training Program Evaluation described here is a fresh use of an evaluation paradigm, an empirical approach to training evaluation. It is a rather unique blend of both positivist and naturalistic methods in order to make evaluation productive, and to ensure a rigorous and systematic framework in analyzing individual program components against recognized standards of measurable program objectives and constructs. The use of an expert team approach to the process is another plus. Experiences at TMI suggest that no one voice can unduly influence the program evaluation outcomes and findings. The process incorporates human research activities such as in-depth interviews and on-site observations linked together, providing a counterpart to intense and hard engineering data and theoretical procedures. In essence, this provides a service to engineering and training managers as well as policymakers. While this process was designed for nuclear utility training evaluation, it holds promise for any critical skills training area in either military or paramilitary environments. It can even prove useful for new and emerging large-scale evaluation needs such as teacher certification.

I submit that The Discrepancy-Based Methodology for Nuclear Training Program Evaluation has the potential to prove useful in many other organizational applications affecting hard and soft sciences. I welcome the comments and inputs from other evaluators and researchers who attempt to implement the methodology in various environments.

Reprinted from *Evaluation and Program Planning* 14, Jeffrey A. Cantor, A discrepancy-based methodology for nuclear training program evaluation, pp. 113–122, copyright 1991, with permission from Pergamon Press, Headington Hill Hall, Oxford OX3 OBW, UK..

- Conclusions must be derived directly from the findings.
- The findings usually add up to one or two conclusions regarding the problem statement.
- The number of conclusions one makes depends on the question asked in the problem statement and the specific questions asked in the sub-problems.
- Avoid statistical terminology in this section. It properly belongs in the findings section.
- Use generalizing language in the conclusion section. For example, one may say, "Procedure X is likely to produce greater levels of achievement in ninth graders"; one may *not* say, "Procedure X will produce greater levels of achievement in tenth graders."
- Conclusions should be supported by overall findings.
- If possible, tie in the conclusions with previous research studies that have been reported in the literature.

To help in the conclusions section, writers often ask:

- What do the findings mean?
- What might have been happening within the conduct of the experiment (environmental factors of the survey, etc.) to account for the findings?
- Why did the results not turn out as hypothesized or expected; or why did they turn out as hypothesized?
- What circumstances accounted for unexpected outcomes?
- What were the shortcomings of the study? Limitations? Was the study too delimited?
- Who can use the results of the study with confidence? (Keep in mind sampling procedures, goodness of fit.)

In summary, describe the theoretical implications of the work or study—and their practical applications. State conclusions clearly and summarize the support for each. Be clear about the significance of the study. In this section, one may become even more creative in thinking about how the findings relate to a professional community.

References. The references section should alphabetically list every published reference cited in the report or manuscript. Each citation should be presented in the appropriate format according to the stipulated guidelines (again, *APA, Chicago*, or other style). Check and double-check that all references cited are referenced.

Preparing your reference list: Most journals stipulate a style. Where this is not specified, consider using APA guidelines. (The references section at the end of this book is a guide based on the APA style for reference citations).

References support the paper and provide the information needed to identify and locate each source. The reference list appears at the end of the paper. It is double-spaced within and between sources and is arranged alphabetically by the surname of the first author. Sources without authors are arranged alphabetically by title within the same list.

Documenting one's sources with reference citations in text: Citing an author's work in the text authenticates the work, indicates the sources of information for readers, and permits others to find a complete reference to the source in the reference list at the end of the article. Every author cited in text must be included in the reference list. To cite an author in text, place the author's surname and the year of publication in parentheses at the appropriate point.

MANUSCRIPT REPRODUCTION

A Checklist to Follow

In all style manual guidelines, certain basic rules apply. First, all manuscripts must be typed and double-spaced throughout. Levels of headings depend on the topic and kind of research reported. Consult the style manual to review the appropriate style of headings. Be consistent throughout the manuscript. Page numbering is consecutive, beginning with the title page, which is number 1, through the last page.

Articles are returned and/or rejected if basic preparation guidelines established by the journal are not followed. In addition, journals require a signed statement of originality and may require a review or submission fee and/or page preparation charge. Refereed journals do not accept manuscripts which have concurrently been submitted to other journals; this is considered an unethical practice. While publication-review time lines do vary, a writer cannot submit the manuscript to two or more journals at the same time. It is customary to await a decision from an editorial board before submitting to another journal.

Generally speaking, the original manuscript is submitted unfastened, except for a binder clip, together with the title page and original artwork. The stipulated numbers of additional copies are included (the journal editor will not assume responsibility for reproduction of the manuscript) without a title page (and no other identification) and including copies of artwork. This ensures a blind review.

A cover letter transmits the entire package. A phone number where the editor can reach the writer during daytime hours should the need arise is included in the letter. It should also indicate that the manuscript has not been submitted elsewhere and that the writer holds the copyright.

NOW WAITING BEGINS

Manuscript Review Time Lines

Henson (1990) discusses his experiences with respect to time lines. A sample of time lines from submission of a manuscript through ultimate accept-reject is given in Table 4-2. The interval from acceptance to publication also varies from journal to journal. Generally it ranges from three months (for quarterly journals) to two years.

In some cases, there is no official statement of journal policy regarding how long a review will take—and editors state that it is really a function of how many manuscripts arrive at any time. In any event, it is suggested that one speak with the editor to get some indication of a decision time line. Journals tend to stay about three editions ahead of publication.

The Review Process

Generally speaking, if a journal editor receives a manuscript which is either in an inappropriate format or on a topic inappropriate to the journal, the editor immediately returns and/or rejects the work. Otherwise, the manuscript is internally processed for review and an acknowledgment letter is sent to the author. There are generally three phases to the review process: (1) editor review, (2) peer review, and (3) decision—acceptance, revision, or rejection.

First, the editor reviews the work for topic appropriateness to the journal. Again, this phase takes a few days to a few weeks.

Next a peer review by a selected or a nominated panel of reviewers takes place. These people are recruited and/or selected by the executive board of the journal. They are usually academics or professionals in the fields of inquiry of the journal.

The peer review phase takes the longest amount of time in the overall manuscript review process. This is due to the difficulty in controlling peer time. A journal editor must stay close to the peer reviewers, set guidelines, and enforce them accordingly to ensure that reviewers read the manuscript and turn it around in a timely fashion. This does not always happen as these people are volunteers with other commitments.

Evaluations of manuscripts often include the following items:

1. Topic is significant to its field and mission (per mission statement).
2. Literature review is sufficient for the topic.
3. Adequate attention is given to the theoretical/conceptual framework.
4. Research questions(s) and/or issues(s) is carefully framed.

5. Research and writing reflect adherence to standards of inquiry appropriate for addressing the questions raised.

6. Conclusions are carefully drawn and supported.

7. Manuscript is well organized and clearly written and adheres to stipulated style guidelines.

8. Manuscript represents a contribution to the body of knowledge in the field.

The Journal of Vocational Education Research uses a standard manuscript review form (Figure 4-10).

Reviewers usually receive a rating sheet to use in evaluating the manuscript. A sample rating sheet used by *The Journal of Research in Education* (JRE) appears in Figure 4-11. Once the manuscript is reviewed by each of the peer reviewers and returned to the editor, the editor considers it in light of each of the comments and decides whether to accept it. Many journals use a point system, simply summarizing the three reviewers' points and accepting or rejecting accordingly.

Then, the journal editor informs the writer of the decision: a rejection with no invitation to resubmit, a rejection with an invitation to rewrite completely according to specific comments of the reviewers (or as summarized by the editor), a conditional acceptance pending a rewrite with specific comments by the editor, or an acceptance.

Again, review times vary. A writer should call an editor if no response is received from the editor after a reasonable time. If a confirmation letter indicating receipt of the manuscript is not received after one month, one should definitely call—to be certain that the manuscript arrived.

Rejection. A writer needs to be mentally prepared for rejection. Refereed journals obviously do not accept every manuscript submitted. Their function is to screen, select, and publish only what they consider consistent with the readership's needs and interests. Writers learn from practice, and by getting reactions they become more proficient.

An author can set up a list of journals in rank order of submission appropriate to topic and writing. If a writer is rejected, it may be possible to find out why through comments from the editor. Consider the comments, revise as warranted, and submit to the next journal on the list. This plan of action can be continued until a writer succeeds in getting the manuscript into print or it is evident that there is an objective consensus that the work is unpublishable.

Acceptance. A writer may be requested to consider some changes or rewriting as a condition of acceptance. Indeed, getting published may mean relinquishing some academic independence. Consider the points of view of other scholars while protecting the integrity of the research. Take the necessary steps through correspondence and discussions with the editor to reach a mutually satisfactory solution. Chapter 5 discusses working with galley proofs and getting the manuscript ready for the press.

Figure 4-10
The Journal of Vocational Education Research **Standard Manuscript Review Form**

JVER MANUSCRIPT REVIEW FORM

MS#_____

Manuscript:_____

_____

Reviewer: _____

Date Sent: _____   Date Returned:_____

I. EVALUATION	Strongly Agree	Agree	Undecided	Disagree	Strongly Disagree	Not Applicable
A. Topic is significant to vocational education.	___	___	___	___	___	___
B. Literature review is sufficient for the topic.	___	___	___	___	___	___
C. Adequate attention is given to theoretical/ conceptual framework.	___	___	___	___	___	___
D. Research question(s) and/or issue(s) are carefully framed.	___	___	___	___	___	___
E. Reflects adherence to standards of inquiry appropriate for addressing questions raised.	___	___	___	___	___	___
F. Conclusions are careful- ly drawn and supported.	___	___	___	___	___	___
G. Manuscript is well- organized and clearly written; adheres to APA style guidelines.	___	___	___	___	___	___
H. Represents a contribu- tion to knowledge about vocational education	___	___	___	___	___	___

II. RECOMMENDATIONS

_____Accept (as is).

_____Conditionally accept, pending minor revisions specified in "Comments" section. No need for reviewers to see manuscript again.

_____Conditionally accept, pending major revisions specified in "Comments" section. Reviewers should conduct a second review.

_____Reject for the moment, but invite resubmission with major revisions as specified in "Comments" section.

_____Reject, but advise submission to some other journal, such as:

_____

_____Reject outright.

Figure 4-10 (continued)

III. **COMMENTS:** This information is very important to the editorial process in insuring that your recommendations are fully understood. Be as complete and specific as possible. Use additional pages if necessary. Your comments will be kept anonymous by name but the content may be shared with the author(s) and other reviewers.

_____

_____

_____

_____

_____

_____

_____

_____

_____

_____

_____

_____

_____

_____

_____

_____

_____

_____

_____

_____

Figure 4-11
A Sample Rating Sheet Used by *The Journal of Research in Education* **(JRE)**

 Journal of Research in Education

JRE MANUSCRIPT REVIEW FORM▪

Date reviewer was sent manuscript: _____
Date reviewed manuscript <u>must</u> be received by JRE Editor: _____
Manuscript Title: (to be completed by Editor):
_____

Return this completed *JRE Manuscript Review Form* <u>and</u> the manuscript to:
> Dr. Jeffrey S. Kaiser, *JRE* Editor
> 529 East Maple Lane
> Mequon, WI 53092
> (414) 241-8347

POINTS Please circle one for each criterion: (3=high; 0=low)

3 2 1 0 Logical coherence and/or methodology

3 2 1 0 Clarity of writing

3 2 1 0 Scholarship

3 2 1 0 Contribution to theory or practice

TOTAL POINTS: _____
NOTE: Manuscripts totaling at least 8 points will be considered for acceptance as is or acceptance after revision.

Additional Reviewer Comments:
Each reviewer is required to make specific recommendations in the section below. This entire sheet, any notations made on the manuscript, and any additional comment sheets the reviewer wishes to add will be forwarded to the author.

_____
_____
_____
_____
_____
_____

Reviewer's summary recommendations:
❑ Publish as is   ❑ Publish with revisions
❑ Not recommended for publication in *JRE*   ❑ Reduce in length and resubmit for
                                 reconsideration as a *Research Brief*

JSK/

* Approved by the Editorial Board & EERA Board of Directors 2/14/90; amended 6/91, 6/92, 11/92

From *The Journal of Research in Education*. Reproduced by permission of The Eastern Educational Research Association, Mequon, WI, 1993.

FINALLY

When asked, most successful writers say that they establish a routine for writing and discipline themselves to sit down and brainstorm on paper—

regularly. One will often be surprised to see how fast ideas develop on paper into a meaningful readable thesis.

These writers do not initially try to polish every sentence and paragraph into finished form. They first draft concepts and ideas. On a second pass-through they refine these ideas (shift paragraphs or sentences), seek precise words and/or sentence structures, and then finally bring the words into a finished form.

A writer will come to know how he(she) works best—on paper, type-writer, or word processor. A computer word processing package will definitely make the job easier and ensure faster production of manuscripts. Some journals will put the manuscript into print faster if it can be delivered to them on disk.

REFERENCES

Cantor, J. A. (1991). A discrepancy-based methodology for nuclear training program evaluation. *Evaluation and Program Planning, 14,* 113–122.

Cantor, J. A. (1990). Job training and economic development initiatives: A study of potentially useful companions. *Educational Evaluation and Policy Analysis,* Summer *12*(2), 121–138.

Cantor, J. A. (1989). A validation of Ebel's Method for performance standard setting through its application with comparison approaches to a selected criterion-referenced test. *Educational and Psychological Measurement, 49*(3), 709–721.

The Chicago Manual of Style, 13th edition. (1982). Chicago, IL: The University of Chicago Press.

Day, R. A. (1988). *How to write and publish a scientific paper,* 3rd edition. Phoenix, AZ: The Oryx Press.

Euster, G. L. & Weinbach, R. W. (1986). Deans' quality assessment of faculty publications for tenure and promotion decisions. *Journal of Social Work Education,* Fall, *22*(3), 79–84.

Henson, K. T. (1990). Writing for education journals. *Phi Delta Kappan,* June, 800–803.

Henson, K. T. (1987). *Writing for professional publication.* Bloomington, IN: Phi Delta Kappa Educational Foundation.

Noble, K. A. (1989). Publish or perish: What 23 journal editors have to say. *Studies in Higher Education, 14*(1), 97–102.

Publication manual of the American Psychological Association, 3rd edition. (1989). Washington, DC: American Psychological Association.

Chapter 5

More about Journals

This chapter will build upon the information provided in Chapter 4. Once a manuscript is accepted for publication, an author is required to work together with the editor and publisher. This will include working with the copyedited versions of the manuscript, galley proofs, and copyright permissions. It is useful to obtain reprints of your published work. Word processing and its effects on the preparation of the manuscript also merit commentary. A few pages are devoted to this activity. This chapter also describes journal article publishing in electronic form and its peculiarities, as well as related journal activity such as refereeing and editing.

WORKING WITH GALLEY PROOFS

Once a manuscript is accepted for publication it needs to be edited and prepared for press. Generally speaking, the journal editor communicates with you regarding receiving the manuscript in paper copy or on electronic medium such as a word processing disk. The latter helps to eliminate errors in typesetting. Whenever possible, it is suggested to provide both a paper copy manuscript and one in an electronic format.

At the final steps of production, proofs are sent from the publisher to the author for final checking, to identify errors in typesetting. *The Journal of Instructional Development* states:

The purpose of proofreading is to make the printed page similar to the edited manuscript. A change made on the proof for a reason other than achieving agreement with the manuscript is an author's alteration. All changes at this stage due to an author's error or omission will be charged to the author. Hence, no changes in content will be entertained.

Editors will usually request several stages of proofreading. Here are some suggestions that may help you when proofreading.

First, look for copy proof errors. Avoid unnecessary corrections. Every change—even a comma—is expensive in terms of both time and money. When a correction is necessary, do the following:

1. Using a colored pen or pencil, mark the location of the correction in the text.
2. In the nearest margin, write the correction or indicate the error using standard proofreader's marks (these can be found in any style manual and in most dictionaries).
3. If material must be added, try to put it at the end of a paragraph. Space limitations may preclude any additions.
4. Give the proofs a literal reading to catch any typographical errors. Have a spouse or friend read the manuscript paper copy as you follow on the galley sheets. A second reading by someone else is recommended.
5. Check all spelling and punctuation marks to catch deviations from the manuscript.
6. Limit changes to identification and correction of printer's errors.
7. Check all tables, figure captions, headings.
8. Refer to the style manual for more detailed information on proofreading galleys or to other style sheets if provided by the particular journal.

Copyright Permissions

When a manuscript is accepted, an author may be requested to assign the copyright to the journal and its sponsoring association or organization. This is intended to safeguard the works contributed to the journal. Begin preparing for the copyright requirement prior to the acceptance of the work. For instance, if an author takes "substantial" quotes or passages or figures and/or graphics from the works of others, the author will need a copyright release (for additional information on a definition of substantial quotes see Chapter 7). A standard format for such a request for permission is contained in Figure 5-1. It takes several weeks or more to obtain such a release (and often a fee is charged); therefore, it is important to do this in advance of receipt of the publication acceptance. Some publishers require receipt of releases before acceptance or copy editing of the manuscript, so begin this process well in advance. Some publishers may allow receipt of releases up to galley proofs. However, the galley proof time line is often very tight (a day or two), leaving no time to obtain permissions.

Figure 5-1
A Request for Permission to Use Copyrighted Material

Jeffrey A. Cantor
25 Judith Drive
Danbury, Connecticut 06811-3443
(203) 748-4096

December 13, 1992

Evaluation and Program Planning
Permissions Department
Pergamon Press
660 White Plains Road
Tarrytown, NY 10591-5153

Attn: Aline Phillips

Dear Ms. Phillips:

I am preparing a textbook tentatively entitled, "A Guide to Academic Writing," to be published by Auburn House (an imprint of Greenwood Publishing Group, Inc) Medfield, MA. The book is to be released on or about Summer of 1993. My book will be approximately 250 pages and will be hardbound. We anticipate an initial printing of approximately 1500 copies. The approximate retail price will be $40. This book is targeted to university academicians and other professionals needing to publish in the academic arena.

May I please have your permission to include the following from the article by myself: Jeffrey A. Cantor. " A Discrepancy-Based Methodology for Nuclear Training Program Evaluation," <u>Evaluation and Program Planning</u>, Vol. 14, 1991, pp. 113-122:

     1.   Article abstract: (see attached copy as it will be included into book).

     2.   Introduction paragraph: (see attached copy as it will be included into book).

     3.   The Model - A Conceptual Framework section: (see attached copy as it will be included into book).

     4.   Conclusion section: (see attached copy as it will be included into book).

in my book and in future revisions and editions thereof, including

Figure 5-1 (continued)

Letter to: Aline Phillips
Permissions Department
Evaluation and Program Planning
c/o Pergamon Press
December 13, 1992
Page 2

    X   nonexclusive distribution rights in the United States and its possessions and Canada in the English language.

    X   nonexclusive distribution rights throughout the world in the English language.

    X   nonexclusive world rights in all languages.

These rights will in no way restrict publication of your material in any form by you or by others authorized by you. Should you not control these rights in their entirety, would you kindly let me know to whom else I must write.

Unless you indicate otherwise, I will use the following credit line:

from: Jeffrey A. Cantor. "A Discrepancy-Based Methodology for Nuclear Training Program Evaluation," Evaluation and Program Planning, Vol. 14; 1991. pp. 113-122: Reproduced by permission of Pergamon Press, Tarrytown, New York 1992.

I would greatly appreciate your consent to this request. At this time I will assume responsibility for the payment of the fee. For your convenience, a release form is provided.

Sincerely,

Jeffrey A. Cantor, Ph.D.

_____

_____ (date)

    I (we) grant permission for the use requested above.

All authors are required to sign a copyright assignment form similar to Figure 5-2 at the time of acceptance of the article. In doing so, the author(s) is stating that the work is not already in publication elsewhere. Generally, authors are extending to the publisher the right to print the work within a specified time frame from the date of the copyright assignment. If for any reason the work does not get into print in that time, you have the right to submit it elsewhere for publication.

If an author is a government employee, that work *may not* be subject to copyright, especially if the employee produced the work in the course of his or her employment. Likewise, if the work is produced on a "for hire" basis, hence, as part of one's employment with a nongovernment employer, an employer's signature *may be* needed as well.

Authors need to be able to establish that they are the rightful owner(s) of the work (as in the case of co-writers), hold the copyright for such work, and have not previously transferred ownership (or any part thereof) to any other person or organization (except, perhaps, as clearly indicated in the work). One must also be able to establish that the work is original and is not copied from some other work.

You are surrendering the right to control the work, inasmuch as the publisher will now control the resale and reuse of the work.

When a writer assigns an article's copyright to a journal, the author should be aware of the constraints thereby placed on the work. You can reproduce it for teaching purposes, can quote yourself in other works, but cannot use it elsewhere without a written release from the journal. Any person desiring to use any part of it will need to obtain copyright permission from the publisher—not from you.

If you use your writing for teaching purposes, you may reproduce or allow reproduction of the article by co-workers, employees, employers, and professional colleagues for individual research and information purposes. Authors may also use the work as a basis for future works. You also retain (generally speaking) patent rights to works describing innovations. For further details see the discussion on copyright in Chapter 7.

Reprints

Once an article has been published, many journals give the author complimentary reprints of the article and give the author the opportunity to order additional reprints at additional cost. These are page-size reproductions of the actual article, bound in a pamphlet size form. The purpose of this activity is to give writers ample copies of their work for distribution to those who request it—or for their own academic (i.e., teaching) purposes. Authors normally receive one or two copies of the actual volume of the journal in which the article appears.

Figure 5-2
A Standard Copyright Assignment Form

Dr. Jeffrey A. Cantor
Associate Professor Lehman College
25 Judith Drive
Danbury, CT 06811-3443

Dear Dr. Cantor:

The Southern Illinois University College of Technical Careers is pleased to have the privilege of publishing in the *Journal of Studies in Technical Careers* your article entitled "Occupational Education and Economic Development: Partnerships that Work".

Whereas the Southern Illinois University College of Technical Careers is undertaking to publish in the *JSTC* a manuscript of which the undersigned is Author of one or more parts, the Author hereby grants and assigns to the Board of Trustees of Southern Illinois University on behalf of the College of Technical Careers all exclusive first publication rights in English in the copyright to the above referenced work. The *JSTC* will refer all requests for permission to reprint the article in part or in entirety to the Author and has no claim on the article beyond the herein specified first publication rights.

The Author guarantees that the article furnished to the *JSTC* has not been previously published elsewhere or, in the alternative, if the article has been previously published in whole or in part, all necessary permissions have been obtained by the Author and forwarded to the *JSTC*. The Author will submit with his/her manuscript the exact wording of credit lines to be utilized with respect to such permissions for publication in the *JSTC*.

The Author of the above referenced article has full power to make this agreement or, in the alternative, that other co-authors have also signed this document, and to accept these terms for publication in the *JSTC*.

If you agree to the foregoing terms, please sign and date this agreement in the space provided below. Please return immediately one signed copy and retain the other for your files.

OFFERED BY:

Susan S. Rehwaldt
Journal of Studies in Technical Careers

ACCEPTED BY:

Date: 2-22-91

Date: 2-25-91

Generally speaking, if someone becomes aware of the work and wishes a copy, the editor will direct the person to the author. Journals rarely make it a practice to reproduce and mail articles to the general public. Depending on the circulation of the journal, the topic, the avenues by which the journal archives its editions, and so on, an author may receive numerous reprint requests.

PREPARING ELECTRONIC MANUSCRIPTS

Electronic Journals

The computer-electronic information age has also come to academic journal operation. Electronic journals are growing in popularity. If you have regular access to a personal computer (PC) and are familiar with the use of such media as electronic bulletin boards, you can envision how an electronic journal operates.

The electronic journal offers many advantages for both the academic author and the journal sponsor. First, the costs associated with production and management of a journal are greatly reduced. There are no printing costs, mailing costs, graphic arts costs, and so on, involved in an electronic journal. Time is saved when editing and transmitting the manuscript from author to editor to referee, which is facilitated by use of a modem. Costs to the academic community to participate in the journal are also reduced.

Printed paper copy journals are often faced with unavoidable delays between the acceptance of research and its actual publication. The peer-review process is also done electronically, speeding the dissemination of information. Thus, by eliminating the printing process and the time needed to mail the journal to subscribers, the author can relay information to readers much faster than through paper publications.

The American Association for the Advancement of Science has recently begun publishing the *Online Journal of Current Clinical Trials*, in an on-line electronic format. Electronic publishing as an emerging technology affords the academic community almost immediate access to often critical information. For instance, the *Online Journal* contains results of research on new and established medical treatments for diseases. Thus, in the case of this publication, the nearly two months saved in the publishing process could affect the lives of many patients. The technology used to transmit the journal was developed by the *Online Computer Library Center* (OCLC), a partner in the venture. This is the first peer-reviewed electronic publication that contains graphs, charts, and illustrations, all of which are becoming available to more writers through electronic publishing.

Electronic journals have been slow to be accepted. Many early attempts at electronic journal operations did not ensure overall quality control via editorial review and blind referee processes. This is changing rapidly. For instance, PSYCOLOQUY, sponsored by the Science Directorate of the American Psychological Association, is an international interdisciplinary electronic forum for BBS-style "scholarly skywriting." It is a magazine publication. All contributors are refereed by members of PSYCOLOQUY's editorial board.

PSYCOLOQUY invites authors to post a screenful of information or very short articles reporting recent ideas or findings on which the author wants peer feedback in the form of interactive "skywriting" with the international psychological community. At the time of this writing, a subscription is free, but an author needs an electronic mail address—or a bulletin board address. PSYCOLOQUY is based at Princeton University's Psychology Department.

Another electronic journal is *New Horizons in Adult Education*, which publishes original research, conceptual analyses, case studies, and book reviews. All work is subjected to a double-blind review by four editorial board members. The journal asks that electronic manuscripts be prepared according to the manuscript style and references outlined in the APA manual, third edition.

Forms of Submission. Electronic journals typically accept manuscripts in the following forms:

1. BITNET
2. Internet
3. On ASCI (the universal computer language) and mailed to the editor on floppy disk
4. Hard (paper) copy to be electronically prepared on acceptance for publication

This journal is electronically transmitted to subscribers' personal computers (via bulletin boards). There is no cost for subscription at the time of this writing since issues are sent electronically to subscribers of the Adult Education Network (AEDNET). Both AEDNET and the journal are sponsored by Syracuse University through funding by the Kellogg Foundation.

Other journals in electronic format regularly make announcements in *The Chronicle of Higher Education*. Check a recent edition for information about where to write to get information about participation. Also, the Association of Research Libraries publishes the *Directory of Electronic Journals, Newsletters, and Academic Discussion Lists*, which is useful for locating such media.

Libraries are able to receive electronic journals in other forms, such as microfiche. Users can search the on-line data base by keywords, subjects, authors, or titles. Articles which are edited or updated after initial publication are highlighted on the screen with a code such as a red dot, alerting readers to check the correction before basing any research on what may be a flawed paper.

Electronic journals are available to readers twenty-four hours a day. Subscriptions to electronics journals often include the software needed to receive the journal on-line, and some permit readers to stay on-line indefinitely.

The economics of electronic publishing indicates that it is the wave of the future. Participation in electronic journalism continues to climb, while the unit cost of electronic publishing continues to decline.

BASICS OF ELECTRONIC DATA MANAGEMENT

It is obviously common practice now to prepare a manuscript on a word processor. The benefits of doing this are enormous. First, authors need only to key in the manuscript once. From then on, any changes, text moves, and editorial work can be done on-screen with minimal effort. Editing can be done expeditiously, and redundancy of work by author and editor limited or non-existent. Formatting and style work become easy. Pagination and folios, running heads, and levels of headings can be automated. Some word processing programs automatically build tables of contents and mark text for indexing. All of this makes an author's job much easier. In some instances, the delivery of the manuscript to a publisher can be done on disk, allowing the publisher's staff to transfer the work into its system electronically, with very little chance of introducing errors into text material. It is becoming commonplace for publishers to request that manuscripts be delivered in electronic form. *WordPerfect* has become the industry standard for manuscript preparation; it has a utility program which runs inside the main program for formatting manuscripts in APA style.

It is wise to select a common and popular word-processing program as it is easier to interface with publishers if they are also familiar with your program. Use the most up-to-date version of the program. Popular programs such as *WordPerfect* also give customer assistance by telephone, to help them overcome problems in using the program.

Basic Requirements

Information from several publishers as well as from the Association of American University Presses, Inc., is presented here for electronic manuscript preparation. Once a decision has been made to prepare and deliver the manuscript on disk, an author should then obtain basic information from the editor. First, find out what kind of system and hardware the publisher uses or can accept from the author. Most commonly, a DOS or MS-DOS system will be acceptable; this is applicable to most IBM and IBM-compatible computers. The other major system one may encounter is the Apple system. Generally, no matter what system an author and publisher have, a systems analyst working for the publisher can make them compatible.

Other information one will need to know is the type of disk medium used. In the DOS environment, the possibilities are 5 1/4 inch floppy versus a 3 1/2 inch floppy disk—with storage density of 360K (kilo bytes), 720K, or 1.4M (mega bytes). Deliver the manuscript on a disk compatible with a publisher's system requirements.

There are a few guidelines handy to keep in mind as the manuscript is prepared electronically. First, maintain at least one set of backup disks in addition to the main disk set. This will prevent loss of work if the first or primary set of disks is destroyed, lost, or damaged.

• Once you begin your work on the computer, stay with one system and one word processing program.

• Set up an electronic filing system which is manageable for you and your editor. Name your files logically: CHAP1, CHAP2, TBLCONTE, APPEND-A, BIBLIO, and so forth. A file name may be as long as seven characters plus a two character extension. Submit a list describing the files along with the disk when you deliver it to your editor.

• The front matter (title page, table of contents, list of figures) each chapter, appendices, bibliography, and index should be in separate files. In the case of scholarly book manuscripts, footnotes and endnotes should be included with the particular chapter file. In programs such as *WordPerfect* they are consecutively numbered within the chapter. An author can command the program to number footnotes and endnotes consecutively throughout the work. However, in preparing electronic book manuscripts, footnotes and endnotes should be in a separate file, consecutively numbered to ease publisher formatting.

• Maintain at least one current duplicate set of disks as a backup, should something happen to the primary set.

There are also some other useful file management techniques to be noted.

• Label files clearly to prevent confusion—for example, "Disk #1, Frontmatter through Chapter 4." This will make work easier. Avoid overloading a disk; free space must be maintained on the disk at least equal to the number of bytes in the largest file on the disk, in order to edit and restore the file on that disk.

• *WordPerfect* and most other sophisticated word processing programs have stylistic formatting capabilities. Keep all formatting to a minimum, so that if the printer needs to download the files to a typesetting program, the formatting commands will not have to be stripped out—a time-consuming process. Because of the differences in command structure of the various word processing programs, unless the publisher indicates otherwise, it is best not to use the word processor's formatting capabilities to deliver the manuscript to the publisher in electronic format. Of course, if the word processing program is compatible with the publisher's system or if one is delivering a "camera-ready" manuscript, the formatting capabilities are both useful and essential.

• Discuss formatting with the publisher before commencing work on the computer. Very often the best solution is to develop the manuscript as one wishes it to look, print the paper copy manuscript, and then remove the formatting commands from each file. *WordPerfect* can do this with global search and delete features and macros.

In general:

• Notes (i.e., footnotes and endnotes) should not be included in the particular file. *WordPerfect* has the capability to accept the note within the page edit screen. However, this can cause problems if the file is to be downloaded into a printer typesetting program. Therefore, discuss with the editor whether notes should be contained in a separate file.

• *All* copy should be double-spaced, *including* the bibliography and notes. Don't provide extra vertical space unless this space is to appear in the book to set off a break in text. Use the wrap-around feature. Use hard carriage returns only where a sentence must end—as in ends of paragraphs, lines of poetry, headings, lists, and chapter titles.

• Do not use any of the spacial features of the word processor such as centering, right-hand justification, and automatic hyphenation. Use hyphens only for compound words. Substitute two hyphens with no space between them for a dash.

• Unless requested by the editor, do not include any running heads. Page numbers should be put in manually, not by the page number feature of the word processor.

• Margins, left and right, should be set at one inch unless you are instructed otherwise. The tab key should be used uniformly throughout the manuscript for paragraph indentation. Everything should be typed paragraph style.

• Use the margin set command for typing extracts. Do not insert hard spaces for indenting.

• Use either a single or a double space after periods, colons, and so on, at the end of a sentence—just do so consistently throughout the document.

• Indicate levels of various headings by using capital and lowercase letters. Various levels of headings are used for chapter titles, major sections of chapters, bibliography, front matter, etc. Discuss a process for coding heading levels with the editor.

• Use the word processor's commands for underscoring, superscripts, italicizing, bold-facing, etc. Use the command from the beginning of the block of text to be treated until the last word of that block.

• For tables, make sure that tabs, not hard spaces, define the columns. Have a clean paper copy of the table for the typesetter to refer to for accuracy.

• Use hard returns only at the end of a block of text, that is, a paragraph.

The message here is to keep the manuscript as simple as possible—avoiding the "bells and whistles" in the word processing program (as recommended by the Association of American University Presses). Type consistently; spell-out numbers; use the same tab settings, page margins, and so forth from chapter to chapter.

Be wary of the program's special features such as spell-check. A spelling check feature cannot detect misused words. It cannot recognize grammatical mistakes. A careful editorial review is essential for these functions.

Once the manuscript is prepared and a paper copy is printed, refrain from making any changes to the disk copy. This will ensure that what is edited on paper will conform to what exists on the electronic manuscript. More and more publishing houses are editing on screen for the sake of saving time and cost. Some word processing programs, such as *WordPerfect*, have editing red-line capabilities, wherein the author can easily see what changes are made or are suggested.

Typesetters can convert the more popular word processing programs into the program used by the publishers for typesetting the book.

Electronic manuscript preparation is similar to paper copy preparation with some noteworthy variations. In its call for manuscripts, the *New Horizons in Adult Education* journal editors (1991) caution that (1) text and references normally underscored instead be typed in uppercase (all caps) letters and (2) written text explanations of concepts and data be used rather than elaborate diagrams or graphics. These cautions prevent possible software incompatibility between author and user systems.

Camera-Ready Manuscripts

In the case of manuscripts which are to be delivered as camera-ready copy, the publisher supplies a "templet" for actual page layout and specific format instructions. Camera-ready copy is generally reserved for scholarly book production (and journal production as well). Usually, an APA or Chicago style format is used; however, the copy is generally single-spaced throughout.

In preparing camera-ready copy, be aware of your printer's capabilities. Dot-matrix and ink-jet printers do not produce suitable "letter quality" copy for book production requirements. Bear in mind that the page is generally reproduced at approximately 83 percent of the size in which you deliver it, and thus some sharpness is lost. You must have access to a high-quality laser printer for the camera-ready copy that you deliver to the publisher.

A WORD ABOUT REFEREES AND REFEREEING

Part of the world of professional writing is working as a journal manuscript reviewer or referee. Active writers in a field are sometimes asked to act in this capacity. Preparation to be a good referee begins as a writer. What writers experience should provide a framework for their later actions. Ideally we all get constructive guidance from referees-reviewers. If not, we should remember the frustration and anger we experience—so that we don't exhibit the same kind of behavior someday when we serve as mentors.

Yes, referees are mentors—experts in fields as well as writing experts. Referees have been chosen to give the journal a quality control process to ensure that only true contributions to a body of knowledge get into print. Sometimes they do this by recognizing worthwhile information in poorly written form. They may then include suggestions to the writer to help produce good copy. The objective of serving as a reviewer-referee is to produce constructive critiques of colleagues' writing. Referees should clearly accept assignments only in those discipline areas where they have the technical knowledge to do a professional job.

Part of the job as a referee is to recognize contributions to the field—versus restatements of prior works. Referees also need to be astute about research methodology and make suggestions where weaknesses are apparent. The goal is to help fellow researchers develop and formulate good work.

Here are some questions which one should ask when reviewing a manuscript:

1. Does the topic make a genuine contribution to the field?
2. Does the research study methodology reflect best practices in the field? Are there sufficient details provided from which to make a judgment about research methods? What suggestions can I make to the writer to clarify or strengthen the study?
3. Have relevant literature sources been referenced? Did the writer take the time to review the literature completely and use the findings appropriately in the study? Has a comprehensive synthesis been incorporated into the manuscript? What suggestions can I make in this regard?
4. Is the thesis clear and convincing? Given a sound research design and study foundation, are clear contributions made via sound conclusions and recommendations?
5. Does the evidence support the thesis? Are the findings well documented and explained in light of the research questions or hypotheses? If not, what suggestions can I make to help the researcher address these issues?
6. Which stylistic considerations need to be addressed?

Remember, we are blind reviewers. While we each may have a good idea of who wrote the piece, especially in fields where the research community is relatively small, or where people are particularly active in special areas, or where we may have seen a presentation or part of the work by the person at a conference, we are not at liberty to make personal contact to discuss the work. Likewise, we must keep our comments confidential—discussing them or the work itself with no one.

Reviewers often can also recommend other journals which may be more appropriate markets for the work if they feel that it merits consideration.

REFERENCES

Adult Education Network (AEDNET). *New horizons in adult education*. (1992). Syracuse, NY: Syracuse University.

American Association for the Advancement of Science. *Online journal of current clinical trials*. (1991). Washington, DC.

American Psychological Association. *PSYCOLOQUY*. (1991). Princeton, NJ: Princeton University.

The Chicago manual of style, 13th edition. (1982). Chicago, IL: The University of Chicago Press.

Association of Research Libraries. *Directory of electronic manuals, newsletters, and academic discussion lists*. (1991). Washington, DC.

Harvard graphics, version 2.3. (1990). Mountain View, CA: Software Publishing Company.

New horizons in adult education. (1991). Syracuse, NY: Syracuse University Press.

Preparing your electronic manuscript. (n.d.). New York: Association of American University Presses.

Publication manual of the American Psychological Association, 3rd edition. (1989). Washington, DC: American Psychological Association.

Wilson, D. L. (1991). New electronic journal to focus on research on medical treatments. *The Chronicle of Higher Education*, October 2, *38*(7), A–27.

Wilson, D. L. (1991). Researchers get direct access to huge data base. *The Chronicle of Higher Education*, October 2, *38*(7), A24-29.

WordPerfect, Version 5.1. (1989). Orem, UT: WordPerfect Corporation.

Chapter 6

Conference Papers and Presentations

The rationale for including conference papers as a topic in a book of this sort is actually quite simple. One of the best methods to begin publishing activity or to expand one's base for publications is provided by conferences. Participation in scholarly conferences has several advantages for an academician. First, it expands one's horizons relating to the academic discipline. Scholars begin to see new avenues for research, new research perspectives and interests, and new opportunities to secure grants.

NETWORKING AND CONFERENCES

Scholars often network at professional conferences to meet new people —other academics with like interests. Conferences provide an opportunity to debate research pursuits. We share ideas, critique, even argue points about each others' work. At a minimum we come away with new ideas, a sense of what others think of our ideas, and, perhaps, lists of others with whom co-writing on topics of like interest is plausible. Very often such relationships open the door to new opportunities. Hence, we gain valuable insight into the publishability of our work.

Professional conferences also enlighten writers about the various publication media in a given field—journals, newsletters, conference proceedings, monographs, and so on—and the organizations that sponsor these periodicals. They also provide an opportunity to meet editors of journals and scholarly presses and learn of practices in and opportunities for publishing.

Successful writers use conferences as an opportunity to expand research ideas into wider topics and areas of interest. It is often desirable (from a funding as well as a scholarship perspective) to explore research opportunities in cross-disciplinary areas. In addition to the conference paper itself, the knowledge gained through participating in the conference can steer a writer in new directions, to new audiences, new kinds of data, or new treatments to test—all of which yield new opportunities for publication. As our world becomes more complex, this venture into new academic areas becomes a necessity.

By attending conferences, we begin to be active in various academic and professional groups, which in turn leads to invitations to serve in roles such as referees or readers for professional journals. As readers for professional journals, we gain insights into how the review process works and what kinds of materials people are submitting for publication.

A scholar need not initially write and present a paper. There are other conference components which are considered legitimate academic professional activities—such as acting as a discussant at a paper presentation session or as a moderator of a session or as the chair of a roundtable session. Depending on the style of conference management, one can be nominated or chosen for one or more of these activities by self-nomination or by nomination by others. An academic obviously needs a background in the topic or area for a discussant role but may need less technical background for chairing or moderating a session.

WHY WRITE A CONFERENCE PAPER?

Most professional academic conferences are sponsored by scholarly organizations—and use a refereed process for accepting papers for presentation at their annual or regional conferences. As such, the papers have academic weight. Additionally, many of these organizations publish the presentation papers in their annual conference proceedings or through other recognized media. Abstracting services seek paper presentations for publication from conference presenters (usually through the conference coordinator).

Many journal manuscripts begin as conference or symposium presentations. Often, much revision must be made to a conference paper before it is publishable as a journal article, as there can be significant differences between them. Conference papers must be developed as presentations to specific audiences—not as technical and detailed manuscripts, which have extensive references and citations (as discussed in Chapter 4).

In the next few paragraphs, sources of information are provided to assist the scholar in identifying conferences appropriate to his or her work.

WHERE TO FIND CONFERENCE OPPORTUNITIES

Sometimes universities and academic departments sponsor or participate in conferences. Undoubtedly someone in the department is active in an appropriate academic society or association. A co-presentation with an associate (perhaps a co-worker) would be a good way to begin. Other sources of information are our alma mater and former professors. Journals in the area of interest can give good leads.

The Chronicle of Higher Education periodically publishes a special edition entitled "Annual Events in Academe." Within this special edition there are listings by headings of several hundred sponsors of meetings throughout the forthcoming academic year, as well as cross-listings of subjects of those meetings. This special edition is published in August, before the start of the academic year. It also contains deadlines for fellowships, grants, papers, and prizes. Typical sponsors include (for illustrative purposes) the Academy of Management, the American Council on Education, Baylor University, the College and University Personnel Association, the Denver Art Museum, and the Employment Partnership. Typical subjects are admissions, business law, community development, dyslexia, and economics. One will also find larger ads placed by various sponsors for calls for papers, calls for proposals, and workshops. This is the single most comprehensive compilation of presentation, grant, and workshop activity currently published.

Another readily available reference source is the *Encyclopedia of Associations* published by Gale Research. The twenty-fifth edition (1991) contains over thirty thousand national and international organizations. These include trade, business, and commercial kinds of organizations, including agricultural, legal, government, public administration, military, public affairs, fraternal interest, religious, hobby, sports, labor unions, associations, federations, chambers of commerce, Greek letter, and fan club organizations. Each entry includes contact information and descriptions of activities including publications, computerized services, and convention schedules. This single publication is an excellent point of reference for learning about an association or society.

Once a decision is made to participate in a professional conference, the next task is to research the policy and requirements of the particular society or association. Protocol is important, as is familiarity with the conference paper proposal format and content requirements, deadline date for receipt, number of copies, costs to attend and present, as well as membership requirements, if any.

For instance, in *The Chronicle of Higher Education*'s, "Annual Events in Academe" section (p. 32) Barry University published a call for papers for the conference "The Global Village: Ethics and Values" (see Figure 6-1). The call requested that interested presenters send a five hundred word abstract of their proposed paper and write in for additional information. In the same issue, Bentley College announced the Ninth Conference on Business Ethics:

Papers should be approximately 15 double-spaced pages and should include a one-page abstract. All pages will be reviewed by a screening committee. All appropriate

Figure 6-1
A Call for Conference Presenters

NATIONAL ASSOCIATION OF INDUSTRIAL
AND TECHNICAL TEACHER EDUCATORS

CALL FOR NAITTE PRESENTATION PROPOSALS

The 1993 NAITTE Annual Meeting will be held from December 3-7, 1993 in conjuntion with the American Vocational Association Convention in Nashville, TN. Proposals for presentations will be considered for inclusion in the program if they are received by February 10, 1993. Each proposal should include a cover sheet and an abstract of the proposed presentation.

The cover sheet should list the

. title of the presentation
. name, affiliation, address, and phone number of the presenter(s).

The abstract should be two to three typed pages and include

. the purpose
. a brief, comprehensive summary of the content of the presentation
. the educational importance of the presentation
. the audio-visual aids required

Consideration will be given to

. Proposals that are conceptual or research and that focus on industrial and technical <u>teacher education</u> or industrial and military <u>trainer training</u> as fields of inquiry.

Five copies of the proposal should be submitted to

. Thomas J. Walker
Temple University
Dept. of Curriculum, Instruction,
and Technology in Education
Ritter Hall, 346
Philadelphia, PA 19122

Founded 1937

From Call for NAITTE Presentation Proposals, 1993 Annual Meeting, reprinted by permission of the National Association of Industrial and Technical Teacher Educators.

and substantive papers will be published in the Proceedings of the Conference. The deadline for submission is October 31, 1991.

An academic with a strong interest in participating in this conference, knowing it was the ninth such conference, would probably research earlier proceedings (and see what kinds of papers were written in preceding years) to learn the format in order to develop a paper accordingly.

WRITING THE CONFERENCE PAPER

The Conference Paper Abstract

Conferences generally require standard formats for paper abstracts. These usually appear as one or two page synopses of the proposed paper and include the following components: the title of the paper (usually less than a dozen words) and each author's name (generally first, middle, and last name) and affiliation(s). Institutional affiliations are typed immediately under each author's name if authors have different affiliations; otherwise, the affiliation follows the authors's names. Next comes the body of the abstract, which varies somewhat, depending on the kind of paper to be presented. The abstract of a research-based paper should briefly describe the purpose of the research, subjects, data collection methods used, analytic procedures employed, and results obtained. The topic's significance to the audience attending the conference should be made clear. Theoretical papers, discussion papers, and program description abstracts should describe the central issue(s) and identify the highlights of the paper and significant conclusions. A panel/symposium abstract should stimulate interest in the topic and attempt to integrate the presentations which constitute the panel or symposium.

The Eastern Educational Research Association (EERA) sponsors a large annual conference. This group calls for abstracts which contain the following components:

• Major objectives and/or focus
• Perspective (theoretical framework)
• Methods and/or techniques
• Data sources
• Results, conclusions, points of view
• Educational or scientific significance of the work

Generally, abstracts should not exceed one to two pages. The EERA strictly limits the abstract to two pages. A separate proposal cover sheet including name, title, affiliation, and phone numbers for each proposer/author is also included.

EERA also sponsors some specialized presentations and symposia which reflect the practices of many societies and organizations. These are special interest groups (SIGs) which sponsor presentations in specialized areas of interest to the members, graduate student research in progress sessions, and distinguished paper sessions by recognized scholars.

Once a proposal has been accepted by the conference review panel, a presenter receives some directions for developing the paper. In general, the following guidelines can help in the presentation of a paper.

Developing the Conference Paper

When writing a conference paper for an organization such as EERA, in the absence of specific preparation guidelines, a presenter can follow standard style guidelines (see Chapter 4 on journal article preparation). EERA does not specify either a format or paper length preference. However, for the Military Testing Association's (MTA) annual conferences, very specific guidance is provided. The MTA publishes annual conference proceedings and wants all papers to be essentially similar in layout, length, and presentation style. MTA's style guidelines are fairly standard for conference papers and can provide a useful guide for a presenter in the absence of specific requirements.

Maximum Length. Some conferences do not specify length requirements. Those who publish the proceedings will set a limit. MTA limits papers to six single-spaced pages, inclusive of text, references, tables/figures/illustrations, footnotes, and acknowledgments/disclaimers. Some organizations may also have standards for type size and font.

Page Format. Text generally should begin on the first page, headed by the title of the manuscript, each author's name and affiliation. The title should be the same as on the abstract. All material should be single-spaced unless specifically otherwise indicated. Many abstracting services prefer single-spaced text for cost-savings reasons. Do not paginate the manuscript; the page numbers are added when the proceedings are assembled.

Image Area. Manuscripts should be prepared in camera-ready form for abstracting and printing purposes. Therefore, a standard 6.5 by 9 inch image area allows for sufficient margins for binding.

Paragraphs. Short paragraphs of reasonable length (approximately 100 words) are best for conference papers. This permits the reader to understand the presentation. Groups of paragraphs may be given short headings with no more than a double space between them.

Illustrations. Good, clear line illustrations, not larger than the page size, can be used to enhance a paper. Reduce tables to save manuscript space. Insert tables and illustrations exactly where they belong in the text of the manuscript. All material (including photographs) must be black and white. Color often cannot be accommodated in photocopy reproduction.

Mathematical Symbols. Insert any special symbols into text either with a word processor or by hand in black ink. Use standard symbols and abbreviations (define these the first time they are used). Number equations and formulae consecutively for ease of reference.

Footnotes. Generally speaking, use footnotes sparingly. When you do include them, place them at the bottom of the page on which they appear. Do not use endnotes unless the conference style specifically calls for them.

References. Use a standard style format to present all references on the last page of the paper.

Acknowledgments and disclaimers. If these are to be used, give the information in the first footnote or at the end of the manuscript. In some specialized areas such as military research and development, it is necessary to secure permissions or clearances before presenting or publishing such work.

Presenters should also take sufficient copies of the paper to the conference for distribution to the attendees. An original is also needed for the conference management to be used for the published proceedings.

MAKING THE PRESENTATION

Despite the fact that we are teachers and academics and accustomed to speaking before a class, public speaking may be difficult for us. How we prepare for our presentation will determine how effective we are in getting our message across to our audience. Through an oral presentation, we will be able to reach a large audience, stimulate ideas and discussion, and gain support for our thesis or perspectives.

A key skill which all presenters need to develop or recall is the ability to project an impression of strength, confidence, and expertise—despite nervousness. Remember such basics as sounding conversational, lively, and spontaneous; do not read the paper to the audience but, rather, deliver it.

Structure of the Presentation

A "rule of three" used in instructional methodology is equally applicable to public speaking:

1. Tell the audience what you are going to tell them.
2. Tell them.
3. Tell them what you told them.

First, introduce the topic in terms of the major objectives of the work. Why did you embark on the project or research? How will it (or the results) affect this audience?

Warm up the audience during the first few minutes of the presentation. If you can do it successfully, be humorous—but, obviously, not offensive. Catch your audience and make them want to learn more about the topic.

After the introduction comes the body of the presentation. Depending upon how much time is available you may need to emphasize the main points. In a fifteen to twenty minute presentation limit the material to no more than two points. Select ideas to present orally which will stimulate discussion. Remember, the written paper will contain the detail—make them want to read it.

Use of Audiovisuals. If at all possible, use supportive media. Overhead projections work well, if large type is used to ensure visibility. Observe the rule of sevens: Do not put more than seven lines of copy on an overhead transparency or slide, nor more than seven words or characters or graphic elements on a line. Seven segments of information is all one can take into short-term memory at one time (see Cantor, 1992). Use professional lettering, not handwriting. Keep to one main point or concept in each visual projection. It is also wise to check the projector and material prior to your turn at the podium. Give out handouts and/or the conference paper if you wish your audience to have such reference material during the presentation.

We can develop very professional appearing overhead projection transparencies using available office equipment. A transparency master can be prepared with personal computer graphics software such as HARVARD GRAPHICS. This software permits a user to design rather sophisticated illustrations or simply present text in various sizes and styles.

Depending on the printer available, one can then print a paper copy of the completed visual artwork—or print the image directly on a transparency film developed for laser printers. The more common procedure, however, is first to produce a paper original in a photocopier and then transfer the image to a piece of transparency film developed specifically for that photocopier.

Once the transparency has been prepared, it should then be mounted into a frame made of hard card stock for ease of handling when talking in front of a group or audience.

Delivery. Practice your presentation several times before the date of the conference until you feel comfortable with the material and can deliver it clearly and within your time constraints. Try to maintain eye contact with the audience. This is best done by using an outline of the paper from which you can talk or discuss, rather than the paper itself. Use *cues* to help you remember what you want to say.

Avoid talking in a monotone—think about voice intonation, gestures, pacing, and pauses. Generally speaking, a fifteen-page paper can be presented in about twenty minutes. Speak clearly and loudly. Avoid pacing nervously or standing frozen behind the lectern. Watch for meaningless noises—ummm's, oks, you knows.

Body language is very important. Use your body. Indicate emotions and attitudes with both facial expressions and intonations. Some presenters use their hands for underscoring—perhaps too much. Judge the impact via audience analysis: read the audience and vary the presentation accordingly.

Relate your topic and information to areas with which the audience is familiar—relate known information to new or unknown information. Make the presentation informative and interesting.

Finally, bring the entire presentation together in a summary of what you told them. End on a high note, leaving the listeners hungry for more information and ready to read your paper. Make sure your audience understands why the presentation is an important contribution to the field, and why you have called it to their attention.

CHAIRING A SESSION

Acting as a conference session chair, discussant, and/or moderator is also an important scholarly activity. The chairperson of a conference session is responsible for monitoring the entire session. Often success depends on the chairperson's ability to manage the session positively. This includes setting the tone, limiting speakers to their allocated time, and organizing and managing the discussion. If there is no discussant scheduled for the session, the chair should also assume the role of discussion leader but is not expected to offer critiques of the papers.

Ensuring Successful Sessions

The leaders of the Eastern Educational Research Association propose the following suggestions to make sessions operate successfully:

1. Arrive early at the session location, check room arrangements, and introduce yourself to the presenters.
2. Organize the presenters, explain how you will monitor their time, and indicate how the discussant (or you—if there is no discussant) will respond to the papers and permit time for open questions and discussion.
3. Call the session to order and introduce yourself, the presenters, and the discussant.
4. Strictly enforce the time limit on each presentation. (Cards or slips of paper indicating five minutes and one minute can be used to advise presenters of the time remaining for their presentation.)
5. Reserve ten to fifteen minutes for the discussant and five to ten minutes for questions from the audience.

6. Monitor the discussion by timekeeping to assure that it is not monopolized by one individual.
7. End the session on time, thank the presenters and the audience, and clear the room for the next session.
8. If the conference provides one, return the completed session report form to the registration desk.

Session Discussants

The discussant is usually provided with and expected to have received and read the papers of each presenter prior to the conference. According to EERA and many other associations sponsoring conferences, the discussant is not obligated to comment on any paper that was not received before the conference deadline, unless the discussant wishes to do so.

The discussant's comments provide a context for those listening to the session's papers, through supportive comments and constructive suggestions. Avoid intimidating and overly critical commentary, which do nothing to support others' professional growth and development. It is more facilitative and intellectually challenging and rewarding to draw together the works of individual authors and to make positive comments and suggestions for further work.

HOW TO PUBLISH A CONFERENCE PAPER

Once a presenter has completed the conference or symposium presentation, the next step is to ensure that the paper is actually published in a retrievable data base so others in the future can locate and access it. In addition to the conference proceedings itself, other potential avenues are open to the presenter. In the field of education ERIC (Educational Resources Information Center) provides such avenues. Much like other archival services, ERIC is a decentralized nationwide network. Sponsored by the National Institute of Education (NIE), it is designed to collect educational documents and to disseminate them to interested practitioners in the field of education. ERIC publishes a monthly abstracted journal, *Resources in Education,* which announces all documents (such as your paper) which it has acquired. These can be published on microfiche from the ERIC Document Reproduction Service.

ERIC: A Brief Description

ERIC operates nationwide to make educational documents available to teachers, administrators, researchers, students, and other interested people. ERIC publishes two monthly abstract journals: *Resources in Education*

(RIE) and *Current Index to Journals in Education* (CIJE). RIE announces all documents that are acquired by ERIC and that pass its selection criteria. These documents are then made available to the public through the ERIC Document Reproduction Service (EDRS).

Advantages of Having a Document in ERIC. ERIC provides many benefits to contributors, including:

- Periodic announcements mailed to the five thousand RIE subscribers
- Publicity promotions for documents written by the author
- Automatic dissemination to over seven hundred ERIC microfiche subscribers
- Availability of the documents to on-line ERIC users, through access to DIALOG or other bibliographic retrieval services
- Continuous availability "in print" through EDRS

ERIC attempts to examine virtually any document dealing with education. Examples of types of materials collected are the following: research reports, technical reports, project descriptions, position papers, speeches, evaluation studies, state of the art reviews, instructional materials, teaching guides, handbooks or manuals, curriculum materials, annotated bibliographies, tests or measurement devices, and statistical compilations.

When a document such as a conference paper is submitted to an ERIC clearinghouse (check a university library for the appropriate clearinghouse for a paper topic), it is reviewed by subject experts for its contributions. Selection criteria employed by ERIC include (1) quality of content—all documents received are evaluated by subject experts in terms of contribution to knowledge, significance, relevance, innovativeness, effectiveness of presentation, thoroughness of reporting, timeliness, and comprehensiveness; (2) legibility and reproducibility—documents must be legible to permit filming; and (3) reproduction release—for each document submitted, ERIC is required to obtain a signed reproduction release form indicating whether it may reproduce the document. Items for which releases are not granted are considered for announcement only if they are available from a clearly documented source. If a work meets these criteria, one is notified of its acceptance into publication. At this point a paper can be considered published.

Similar abstracting services exist in other disciplines. As indicated in Chapter 2, library abstract guides can provide the information retrieval and archival sources in any discipline area.

IN CLOSING

Conference presentations can be a useful way to get involved in publishing or to extend an academician's publication activity into new areas and directions. By becoming involved in one or more professional associations or societies potential writers can derive substantial scholarly benefits.

REFERENCES

Annual events in academe. (1991). *The Chronicle of Higher Education*, August 15, p. 32.

Cantor, J. A. (1992). *Delivering instruction to adult learners*. Toronto, Ontario, CAN: Wall & Emerson.

The Chicago manual of style, 13th edition. (1982). Chicago, IL: The University of Chicago Press.

Eastern Educational Research Association. (1989). *Annual conference call for papers & symposia—1989*. Oswego, NY.

Encyclopedia of associations, 25th edition. (1991). Princeton, NJ: Gale Research.

Harvard graphics, version 2.3. (1990). Mountain View, CA: Software Publishing Company.

Military Testing Association. (1992). *Abstract preparation for the annual conference of the Military Testing Association (MTA)*. Washington, DC.

U.S. Department of Education, Office of Educational Research and Improvement (1986). *Directory of ERIC information service providers*. Washington, DC: U.S. Department of Education.

WordPerfect, Version 5.1. (1989). Orem, UT: WordPerfect Corporation.

Chapter 7

Developing Grants and Contracts

Colleges and universities look very favorably upon grant and contract writing for research and development. Well written grant and contract proposals will result in increased funding for the university. This funding will support graduate students, adjunct faculty, program development, special events, and administrative overhead costs. Often, it also brings in new equipment (i.e., computers, scientific apparatus, laboratory furnishings).

WHY WRITE FOR GRANTS AND CONTRACTS?

Grant and contract proposals, even if not funded, call the college's or university's resources—its faculty talents, research interests, and university support capabilities—to the attention of a funding organization or government agency. This information and exposure often result in unsolicited grants of money (those for which no proposal is necessary; the organization merely directs funding to the university on written acceptance). Oftentimes a limited number of colleges or universities are invited to submit proposals for special areas of interest when a funding organization or agency becomes aware of their unique capabilities.

Faculty become knowledgeable in a new area of inquiry as a result of the research necessary to develop and write a grant proposal. These writing activities broaden the overall publishing ability of the individual faculty member.

Grants and contracts provide financial support for faculty publications. Those who actively publish can fully appreciate the cost involved in getting one's work into print. Grants can offset the costs of writing by providing the money to hire research support, such as graduate assistants, and administrative support.

Sometimes it becomes necessary for a university or scholarly press to seek subsidy funding—called subventions—to offset the cost of putting a market-limited work into press. These subventions might come directly from the author or from subsidies received from the press's sponsoring institutions. While subventions may typically be only two thousand to five thousand (Luey, 1990), these monies will probably amount to the potential royalties gained from such a work.

The difference between a grant and a contract for research and development is quite simple—yet important to understand. A contract for research and development, usually awarded by a federal governmental agency, is an agreement to produce a specific product. These opportunities for free and creative expressions of ideas are severely limited. A government project officer always directs a researcher's work, closely monitors progress, and decides how the project will be developed. Contract researchers are held to delivery dates, project and product specifications, and budget parameters. In the end, these works may be in the public domain.

A grant is a "gift" of money which is awarded to faculty to explore their academic pursuits, essentially in an undirected manner. The only constraints are budget and time limits. The rights to publication are for the most part the researcher's.

HOW TO GET STARTED

The first step to becoming a successful grant and/or contract writer is to become familiar with funding opportunities. Speak to the college grant development officer. This person should be able to provide guidance to various organizations (public and private) that may have an interest in receiving a proposal for your research. Faculty can also learn of requests for proposals (calls for grant and contract proposals) from governmental or private organizations. Most colleges have a distribution list for faculty or others interested in receiving these announcements. Several computer software programs can help match research topics to potential funding sources. Generally when faculty alert the grant officer of their interests they can to be placed on various mailing lists.

For instance, the City University of New York has a collective bargaining "agreed-upon fund" for faculty research. As in many other colleges and universities, this fund is accessed via internal grant competitions. Each fall, a competition period commences with a call for proposals open to all faculty. Categories of funding opportunity are specified. A limited competition is also available to junior faculty only, to allow these colleagues opportunities to establish their research and publishing track records. A peer review panel is established for each specific category or area. Many colleges and universities have similar internal grant funding sources. Become aware of these opportunities.

Published Guides

There are numerous commercially published guides to grant funding opportunities. Weekly information pertaining to grant funding opportunities is published in *The Chronicle of Higher Education*. Another viable source of current information is the *Federal Register*.

The Federal Register. *The Federal Register* publishes daily releases of federal funding opportunities and other federal projects which create research and development activities and academic study opportunities. Most university grant offices and libraries receive both of these periodicals.

Commerce Business Daily. A third, and perhaps lesser known daily publication containing contract funding opportunities (usually not grants) is the *Commerce Business Daily* (CBD). This publication contains daily announcements of federal purchasing requirements. By federal statute, the U.S. government publishes their competitive bid requests (opportunity) one month before reviewing bid requests and making selections. Several categories in which competitive studies and research projects appear can be of interest to academics, such as management consulting and training services. The CBD is sold by the U.S. Department of Commerce in Washington, D.C. Most libraries have a subscription. Make it a practice to review as many of these as possible on a regular basis. It is wise to keep in touch with the contracting offices in those federal agencies for which one has an interest in providing research and development services.

Foundation Grants to Individuals. *Foundation Grants to Individuals* is the most comprehensive listing available of private U.S. foundations which provide financial assistance to individuals. The seventh edition lists over thirty-two thousand active private grant making foundations. The foundation center has identified these organizations as conducting ongoing grant making programs for individuals. Grants can be provided for a variety of purposes including scholarships, student loans, fellowships, foreign recipients, travel internships, residencies, arts and cultural projects, and general welfare. *Foundation Grants to Individuals* is intended to be both a grant seeker's guide and a reference tool for those individuals interested in foundation sponsorship.

Other Publications of Interest

Several other resources which are carried by most research libraries are recommended. In the area of federal funding consider the following:

Guide to Federal Funding for Governments & Non-Profits. This guide is published by Government Information Services of Arlington, Virginia. It is published annually with monthly updates and contains new articles on legislative developments in Congress in addition to descriptions of over two hundred federally funded programs. These programs are available to state and local governments and to non-profit organizations. To respond to one of these programs, a researcher must be professionally associated with either a non-profit organization or a university—or possibly a research-based foundation. Topics covered include housing, pollution control, homelessness, and economic development, to name but a few.

There are other sources of government information directly obtainable from the federal government. For instance, according to Meador (1986), the federal and many state governmental agencies provide information about sponsored research in various areas such as business, energy, and technology. Some data bases and sources that may best meet one's particular need are listed in Table 7-1.

Additionally, consider the following sources.

Popular Government Sources. The National Endowment for the Humanities—Division of Research Programs supports production of scholarly works and documents in all humanities fields. The National Endowment for the Arts—Literature Programs supports publication of fiction and offers assistance to non-profit literacy small presses specializing in creative literature. The National Library of Medicine—Publication Grant Program supports not-for-profit publication projects of all kinds in biomedical sciences and health care. The U.S. Small Business Administration, Office of Advocacy sponsors the Small Business Financial Research Program for the purpose of promoting research on financing small business and relevant public policy issues. In 1988 five awards in the ten thousand to fifteen thousand dollar range were made.

Special grants for publishing from such sources as the National Historical Publications and Rewards Commission may be available. This federal agency was established to assist both public and private organizations to put documents of historical interest into print and archives. The funding can be used for research assistance, editorial and reference work, typing, copy editing, reproduction work, and so forth; grants have ranged from $2,500 to $170,000.

Other Published Sources. The *Annual Register of Grant Support* is an annual volume that lists and details the grant support programs of government agencies, public and private foundations, corporations, community trusts, unions, educational and professional associations, and special interest organizations. The volume covers a broad spectrum of interests from academic and scientific research, project development, travel and exchange programs, and publication support to equipment and construction grants, in-service training, and competitive awards. Each listing contains information

Table 7-1
Data Bases

Subject	Source
Energy-related research and information	U.S. Department of Energy Technical Information Center Oak Ridge, Tennessee
Energy reference services	U.S. Department of Energy National Emergency Information Center Washington, DC
Business and commerce reference services	U.S. Department of Commerce Library Washington, DC
Technical reference and bibliographic services (free and fee-based)	Science and Technology Division, Reference Section Library of Congress Washington, DC

pertinent to the organization, including details of type, purpose, duration of the grant, amount of funding available, and eligibility requirements. The number of grants made in the previous year is usually also reported.

The Foundation Directory is a standard reference work for information about non-governmental grant making foundations in the United States. The eighth edition contained over 3,363 foundation entries. The foundations are grouped alphabetically by state. The index of fields of interest separates foundations with national or regional giving programs from those with local interests. Each entry gives the full legal name of the foundation, its address and telephone number, establishment legal information, donors, purpose and activities, assets, grant amounts, number of grants made within the preceding year, together with foundation points of contact and application information.

Research Centers Directory, published by Gale Research Company, is a guide to university-related and other non-profit research organizations in areas such as agriculture, business, conservation, law, life sciences, mathematics, area studies, physical and earth science, social sciences, and humanities. Listings include research institutes, centers, foundations, laboratories, bureaus, experiment stations, and other non-profit organizations. Data covered include formal name of the organization, affiliation, address, director, year activity began, present funding status, principal fields of research, media in which research results are published, serial or periodic publications of the activity and their frequency of issue, and recurring seminars, conferences, colloquia, and short courses conducted or sponsored by the activity and whether these are open to the public or are limited in attendance.

Directory of Research Grants, published by Oryx Press, is another tool for identifying grant funding sources. It is arranged by subject areas and includes a description of the program, deadline dates, address, telephone number, amount of grant possible, and Catalog of Federal Domestic Assistance Program number. Oryx feels that this directory also serves the scholar by providing mental stimulation as to kinds of research possible, funding opportunities, and the like.

Also consider . . . Other sources for financial assistance are independent foundations, community foundations, and company-sponsored foundations. There are numerous other funding opportunities in specialized areas and disciplines. In addition to the government, private foundations sponsor academicians in furthering scholarship. For instance, in the areas of naval training and human resource development, the U.S. Navy's Office of Naval History has annual calls for research grants using non-appropriated funds (the Vice Admiral Edwin B. Hooper Research Grant Program). Grants of up to twenty-five hundred dollars are intended to assist scholars in researching and writing books or articles by helping defray the costs of travel, living expenses, and document duplication related to the research process.

The National Center on Adult Learning (NACL), Empire State College of the State University of New York, puts out an annual call for practitioner-based research proposals in the area of adult education and learning. The 1991–1992 competition was supported, in part, by a grant from the W. R. Kellogg Foundation. Proposals are invited from academics and practitioners alike on a broad range of topics. Award winners are also considered NACL Fellows and invited to an annual meeting to present their research, with expenses covered by the grant.

How about Specialized Organizations?

The Aspen Institute sponsors the Nonprofit Sector Research fund to encourage basic and applied research in the non-profit sector. Grants up

The International Foundation of Employee Benefit Plans grants funds to individuals for research on employee benefits through its Postdoctoral Grants for Research Program. These grants are in amounts up to ten thousand dollars.

A look at the September 30, 1991, *Chronicle of Higher Education* discovered myriad other funding opportunities, including the following:

- The Society of Historians of American Foreign Relations Myrna L. Bernath Book Prize of twenty-five hundred dollars for the best book published by a woman in the areas of U.S. foreign relations, transnational history, international history, peace studies, cultural interchange, and defense or strategic studies.

- The Myrna L. Bernath Research Fellowship of twenty-five hundred dollars for females to undertake historically based research.

- The Carter G. Woodson Institute for Afro-American and African Studies at the University of Virginia announced the availability of residential research fellowships in Afro-American and African studies. Post-doctoral fellowships for one year carry a stipend of twenty-five thousand dollars.

- The United States Agency for International Development Indo-U.S. Science and Technology Fellowship Program announced a request for proposals for scientific research opportunities in India in 1992. U.S. scientists wishing to conduct collaborative work with Indian scientists in the fields of atmospheric/environmental science, biological science, biotechnology, chemistry, computer software, electronics, forestry, et cetera, could apply. Stipends for three to twelve months with travel paid are awarded.

OK—Now What?

After identifying an appropriate grant source(s), the next step is to establish personal contact with that organization. Discuss your research ideas and establish whether an interest exists in the organization and whether it fits the organization's funding missions. At this time you will also gather specific details about form and formats for the grant proposal development and application.

Funding organizations publish applications and information packages that describe their application procedures, review processes, various funding programs (i.e., small grants for exploratory research, usually to seventy-five hundred dollars), fellowship programs, and time lines and submission dates. Once a grant (or contract) source is identified, contacts are made, and required paperwork is reviewed, one is ready to develop and write the grant proposal.

DEVELOPING AND WRITING GRANT PROPOSALS

The development of a grant proposal requires the same concise and clear writing style described in the previous chapters. The specifics of developing a contract proposal are discussed later in this chapter. Perhaps the major difference between a grant proposal and a research report or journal article is that the grant proposal is a sales document. A researcher as a proposal writer is trying to sell an idea or concept. This writing must be convincing and persuasive. It needs to convince the sponsor that one is proposing to solve important problems. Arguments supporting one's research ability —competence, background, facilities, and available support personnel— should be made.

Generally, issues of appropriate presentation formats are addressed in the proposal instructions. In unsolicited proposals (those which you submit to an organization which has not announced a specific competition or program) the general format discussed here should suffice. However, be aware that certain organizations, especially federal agencies, mandate particular formats and number of pages count! Writers cannot do it their own way.

When a proposal arrives at the funding organization it is reviewed by a panel. Submitters are usually required to submit multiple copies as specified in the grant application instructions. Review panelists are not necessarily familiar with the technical information or subject matter in the proposal. Adapting the proposal terminology to a more commonly used language and/or defining specialized terms is very important. As indicated in earlier comments, avoid abbreviations and acronyms. One way to ensure readability is to ask a colleague to read and critique the proposal. The most favorable reviews are for proposals that are succinct and to the point. Lengthy narratives lose points. Use graphics to summarize (and reduce) text whenever possible.

The following are the major components of a proposal:

- Cover letter
- Title (cover) page; table of contents; abstract
- Introduction; background
- Statement of problem; need for the study
- Objectives of the research
- Methodology (description, procedures, and time lines)
- Evaluation processes (quality control and organization)
- Dissemination and utilization of research
- Personnel—vita (including staff)
- Facilities and support
- Budget
- Bibliography and references

A description of each of these components follows.

Cover Letter

It is important to identify a specific organizational point of contact early in the research on the funding organization. It is useful to meet this person personally to learn as much as possible about the organization's funding goals and interests in your research. A personal meeting also establishes name recognition from this point of contact. The cover letter should now relate to this previous meeting and serve as a letter of submittal of the proposal. Make it friendly, cordial, and business-like. It serves as a primary marketing document to introduce the project or concept to the review panel. Do not restate the case—merely wet their appetites to read the proposal.

Title Page, Table of Contents, and Abstract

The title page is usually on a form provided by the funding organization. Items usually included are the following:

- Title of your project
- Principal investigator; your name(s) and title(s)
- Organizational affiliation(s)
- To whom submitted
- Project duration
- Proposed budget totals
- Date of submission

The project title should be as descriptive as possible, emphasizing the actual goal of the project. The title should "grab and sell." Give it appropriate attention.

A table of contents should give the reviewers a concise overview of the proposal and an easy means to walk back and forth through the proposal.

An abstract is also a most important component of a research proposal. It must sell the uniqueness of the project and its anticipated contribution to the field it represents. All too often the attention a proposal ultimately receives from a review panel is determined when these people read the abstract. If they're sold mentally on a proposal's merits by the abstract, it usually gets a positive reaction and further consideration by the panel.

Introduction and Background

The introduction and background of the proposal must tell the readers and reviewers what the project is all about. An introduction identifies who the researchers are, what they are proposing to do, and why they are qualified to do it. This section is very important in an unsolicited proposal as these proposals need not be read any further if this initial question does not engage the primary decision maker—the reader. In as few words as possible state the goals of the project, the researcher's unique qualifications (previous research and accomplishments) to undertake it, and the organizational resources. The background paragraphs should summarize previous research and work in the field, where this project fits in, what specific questions remain unanswered, and what the researcher expects to accomplish and contribute to the body of knowledge.

Statement of Problem and Need for Study

The statement of the problem must tell the reader specifically what is involved and why. Summarize what you plan to investigate and its implications to the field. Keep this section to a few well structured paragraphs.

Objectives of the Research

What is proposed to be accomplished is the need or scope of the problem (as stated previously). An objective must be specific—and limited to manageable problems. Objectives can be stated as research questions or hypotheses, depending on the proposed study methodology. Researchers develop the objectives in a manner which describes the benefits to be derived by the academic or social community as an outcome of the project. Objectives must be measurable: concrete and attainable. Carefully stated objectives give all concerned, the grantor and grantee, check-off points or milestones for the project.

Methodology—Description, Procedures, and Time Lines

The description of the project is a central element that details how the objectives will be achieved within a stipulated project time frame. The description includes a work plan, methods, procedures, rationale, and quantitative projections of accomplishments. The work plan lists each objective and discusses it in terms of what will be done to address the objective and when. If the methodology is based on a pre-developed model, be as descriptive as possible, citing a literature base. Describe the genesis of the method and why it provides an appropriate foundation for your proposed research.

Methods for data sampling, collection, and analysis (including instrumentation design and validation) should be described. Ethical considerations such as data security and subjects to be used should be included. If historical data or records retrieval are involved, how will you access these data? If clearances are needed, describe how such permission will be secured.

Time lines, as a form of management by objectives, should be included. They demonstrate that you understand the realities of the project and assure the grantor that the objectives of the project can be achieved. Each objective should be enumerated on the time line chart, together with starting and ending dates, personnel to be assigned, and hours each person will devote to each objective and task.

Evaluation Processes: Quality Control and Organization

Quite often a major barrier to accessing funds for individual grantees such as college professors is that a funding agency has no guarantee that the individual can complete a project as promised. It is through a well conceived evaluation process that one can reassure the grantor of quality control measures and organizational support mechanisms as a check and balance on your project.

The City University of New York has a research foundation policy and procedures manual. The policies and procedures outline how funding is accounted for; how research assistants are hired, monitored, and terminated; what can be purchased and how, according to individual grant budgets; how grant project time lines are monitored; and other uniform processes which have been developed to assure responsible grant monitoring for quality control. The research foundation has an organizational structure to support a principal investigator which dovetails with the university's administration and hierarchy.

A reporting system is very important and should be described specifically in the proposal. If the funding is a performance contract rather than a grant, this reporting system and schedule of deliverables are most important. In this case, a process for addressing contracting concerns also must be stipulated.

Dissemination and Utilization of Research

The dissemination and use of research component of the proposal describes how the researcher will share study findings with the academic and/or professional community or other potential end users. Describe plans to share this information with others—publications, presentations, monographs, or any other possible media. Provide examples from past projects. Faculty often refer to their vita or publications list. Very often this part of a grant proposal is overlooked or minimized. Grantors view this activity as essential. A writer's willingness to provide a plan of use and dissemination is received positively. For instance, in the U.S. Small Business Administration Small Business Financial Grants award, it is stipulated that the award holder is responsible for supplying the government with a final report summarizing the research effort.

Personnel: Researchers' Qualifications

Proposal writers need to include a descriptive resume for all researchers and staff who will be committed to the project. This should be a succinct resume—not a standard academic curriculum vitae. This document is intended to give the grant organization's staff a statement of qualifications to perform the intended research activity. The only information of importance to the organization is the specific talents, educational preparation, and experience related to the project under consideration. Present these facts in a clear and concise manner.

The following items are usually included in a research proposal's resume:

1. Name, address, and phone number
2. Education, colleges attended; degrees received, and fields of study
3. Experience—a work record with some description of positions and responsibilities
4. Publications list pertinent to project only
5. Professional roles and activities, special assignments, presentations, workshops, or other activities related to the project
6. Professional memberships
7. Professional skills as related to the project with documentation of ability to perform project tasks

Again, do not attach a standard curriculum vitae. Rewrite a resume which highlights the specific talents and requirements stipulated in the grant request for proposal (RFP). Use the categories called for (i.e., educational preparation, work experience, publications). Adhere to page limitations imposed for the resume in the RFP. If none is specified keep the resume to a maximum of three to four pages—trimming publications to only the most recent or relevant, and work experience to the most relevant.

Staff resumes are prepared in the same manner. Include a descriptive link between personnel and research objective and project a task matrix to describe staff relationship to the project and to each other. Do not omit anything that is relevant to the project and establishes the staff's credentials for working on the project. On the other hand, do not include the extraneous and irrelevant.

Facilities and Support

If facilities and support such as clerical and data processing are an integral part of the project, these resources should be described. A letter of support from the institution should be included when pledging university support as part of a proposal. Often proposals are submitted through the university research foundation, which has "boilerplate" or specific pre-written material describing their available supportive services. For projects requiring such support (computer analysis, media, library, clerical, word processing, accounting), unless one can document guaranteed access, a staff's unique talents alone will not convince a funding agency that their money will be well spent.

Budget

A detailed description of the proposed project budget must also be submitted. Usually, a required budget format is provided by the grantor. This will generally take the form of specific forms which you must complete (sometimes with backup data to support them). At a minimum, you will need to provide salary information for all researchers and staff. Salaries also require mandated fringes (usually in a percentage form) based on university overhead statistics. Work with the grants officer to prepare this portion of the budget.

In many cases, salary of the principal investigator (you) cannot be directly paid. That is, one sometimes cannot draw money directly—other than a portion of one's summer session salary. Consult local authorities to determine in detail how one may be compensated for research and development project work. Often faculty write in staff salaries for students as research associates.

Other direct research costs are usually permissible, such as paper goods (stationary), computer software, possibly computer hardware, work of specialized consultants, travel, telephone, postage, and manuscript preparation.

Be careful to state the budget carefully and document all expenses. Be prepared to adjust it if and when the grantor offers less than the requested amount in a conditional award.

Bibliography and References

Include, as an appendix, a detailed bibliography to support the proposal. This demonstrates a certain basic knowledge of the literature; it also demonstrates some preliminary work by the researcher in investigating the topic. Grantors want to see comprehensive understanding by responders to RFPs or submitters of proposed research. It indicates that one is truly trying to add to a body of knowledge rather than just to attract money and reinvent existing knowledge and technology.

The Grant Review Process: Follow-up on
Grant Submissions

Grants are made through a peer-review competitive process much like that of refereed publications. Depending on the kind of organization, these reviewers may be drawn from an academic discipline, from industry or academia, and sometimes from the international community. The granting organization establishes a peer-review panel to submit the proposal to a rigorous analytical review in terms of the organization's criteria. Highlights of a typical proposal evaluation review (Research Foundation of CUNY) are as follows:

1. At least *three* independent signed reviews for each proposal are required, of which *one* must be extramural to the university.
2. No internal reviewer may be from the applicant's campus.
3. Applicants for an award *may not review* others' proposals, although they may serve on a different panel.
4. All internal reviews are made on a standard internal signed evaluation form. Extramural reviews must be on the standard extramural review form.
5. Panel members are encouraged to select extramural reviewers specializing in that particular area of research.

DEVELOPING AND WRITING CONTRACTS

Much of what has been discussed for grant proposals applies to responding to contract requests for proposals (RFPs) as well. However, the specific proposal response requirements for RFPs, most of which are to the federal government, require some additional discussion.

While contract work can be very restrictive in terms of creativity, the return on investment can be very great. In many university settings, grant money can only be used by a principal investigator for staff (research assistants, typists) salaries and for supplies (paper, telephone, travel).

Research and development contracts can be handled differently. In some cases faculty incorporate as a small business and bid on a contract. On receiving the award they can then draw salaries from the small firm, as consultants or part-time staff researchers. Additionally, contracts can be a source of funding for equipment (laboratory equipment and computers) that is otherwise too costly for some colleges today. Become familiar with RFPs. Federal requests for proposals are uniform across the government, and all contain the following elements:

1. A Statement of Work (SOW): The SOW section describes the work which the agency wishes to have performed. It is specific in terms of tasks to be performed. A researcher must address the approach that will be taken to perform each task, as well as staff qualifications and experience in

dealing with each task. A typical SOW as shown in Figure 7-1 details the requirements of the government, personnel qualifications, research design, cost constraints, and contractor responsibilities. It also gives specifics on what (data, materials and/or support) the government will furnish to the bidder to do the work.

A. A time line for work completion: This describes the time constraints on job performance. The government requires that proposers demonstrate how they will manage the contract to ensure timely completion of the work within the time frame specified.

B. Labor requirements: This section requires specific information about professional, technical, and clerical support. The RFP usually specifies educational requirements, percentages of time on project for each position, and background and experience requirements related to task and to the kind of work environment. Proposers should address each of these conditions; often one needs to locate and identify other people to complement a team in the proposal.

2. Management: This part of the RFP requirements requires proposers to describe how they will manage the entire contractual work effort and ensure high-quality performance. It usually calls for monthly or quarterly progress reports, describing progress to date task by task in terms of the time line. Look clearly at what responsibilities the government has to support contract performance, including turnaround times for drafts.

3. Cost: This is the one section of the RFP that will leave you guessing! The government looks for the best buy for its money. Proposers need to do some homework to determine a reasonable and competitive price to bid or charge the government. Determine (1) the length of each task— sometimes given in the RFP; (2) the kind of professional labor, and proportion of that labor category for each task; (3) the customary salary rates for each kind of labor; (4) other direct costs such as travel, materials, and computer time and amounts of each required to do the job. Next, consider the overhead rates created by the proposing firm, an aggregate of rent, phone, light, heat, and so on, and the percentage of these to be charged to the contract. Finally, what about profit? Usually 3 to 8 percent of the subtotal is an acceptable profit or fee.

See whether the contract is a fixed-price type or a cost-plus-fixed-fee (CPFF) type. A fixed-price contract requires proposers to perform to the government's satisfaction despite numbers of redrafts of documents or additional hours spent on data collection, travel, et cetera, until the job is done—and for no additional money. CPFFs sometimes allow for "overruns" or renegotiation should unforeseen circumstances arise.

Remember Freedom of Information (FOI). One ace in the hole in bidding for government work is the ability to glean information about past services acquired by a government agency through the Freedom of Information Act. On written request to the Freedom of Information officer in a

Figure 7-1
A Typical SOW

SECTION B - SUPPLIES/SERVICES/PRICES

Background

The Office of Advocacy of the U.S. Small Business
Administration announces the initiation of a Small
Business Financial Research Program. Awards are for the
purpose of promoting research on financing small business
and relevant public policy issues. Approximately five (5)
awards in the $ 10, 000- $ 15, 000 range will be made.
Proposers are to specify the cost of the project and how the
money will be allocated among direct support for a scholar,
research assistance, overhead, etc. Proposals requesting
project assistance, marketing studies, management methods
development, or business assistance will be considered
NON- RESPONSIVE. Proposals that exceed five (5) doubled-
spaced typewritten pages or that request more than $15,000
will also be considered NON-RESPONSIVE.

Small businesses have special financing concerns
because they often cannot obtain long term debt or equity
in most traditional financial markets. This constraint
requires small firms to rely on trade credit and bank
credit as major sources of short terms debt and to
obtain new capital from the entrepreneur's own funds,
informal investors, venture capitalist, and retained
earnings of the firm. As an alternative to raising debt
and equity, small firms sometimes convert liquid assets into
cash through factoring accounts receivable and warehouse
inventory. Securitization of assets is a developing method
for small firms to liquidate assets.

Furthermore, traditional financial markets are likely
to be supplemented by new markets and innovative services
that evolve to service the unsatified needs of small
business. In some instances services that are now unbundled
by providers will be unbundled to appeal to small firms.

Figure 7-1 (continued)

SECTION C - DESCRIPTION/SPECIFICATIONS/STATEMENT OF WORK

C-1 - Purpose/Requirements

The Small Business Financial Research Program is a
solicitation for fresh ideas for applied research on small
business finance and economics. In some instances empirical
research will not be possible because of time and data
limitations. Important theoretical and non-empirical
analytical studies might be proposed for the Program.
Funded projects are not expected to involve the collection
of significant amounts of business data. Case studies
involving interviews of 10- 15 firms may be proposed.
Development of theoretical models may be a useful
alternative to analyze an important small business
financial issue.

Example of types of projects that might be of interest
includes: the development of new sources of funds for
start- up of new business, effects of changes in interest
rates on small- business development, analysis of venture
capitalist's investments in small firms, relationships
between usage of various sources of funding small firms,
effects of public programs to support small business,
relationships between small business performance and local
economic activity innovation, and firms size, and effects
of changing financial markets on small firms.

Proposals must clearly state the objective, methodology,
and specific policy issues to be addressed by the
contemplated research. A resume of each research
participant should be attached to each copy of the
proposal. To allow for timely evaluation, proposals are
limited to five (5) double-spaced typewrittem pages, plus
resumes.

governmental agency you can find out the exact price the agency has paid in the past for similar work. In fact, one can often access proposal information as well. Proposers need to request specific contractual information from past competitions. One cannot ask for general information.

4. Specific proposal instructions: The agency details the specific formats and kinds of information (and page limits) for your proposal. Follow their instructions carefully—including page length, typeface, number of copies, and submission times, dates, and places carefully or you will be disqualified.

The government usually takes three to nine months to make an award. Proposers may be asked for additional information or for a best final price prior to a final decision.

Some Words on Evaluation Criteria

Applications are judged on the following:

1. Scholarly or creative merit, originality, and significance of the proposed research.
2. Ability of the applicant to perform the work successfully. When considering previous research experience, the reviewers take into account the fact that junior faculty are often unable to present a long record of research experience. However, an inadequately prepared proposal, even if submitted by a well established investigator, will not be funded.
3. Progress reports and publications (if any) in the case of renewal applications.

What If My Project Is Not Funded?

Be ready to pursue other avenues. Federal statistics indicate that you will probably not be successful on the first submission. When responding to a federal RFP be aware that less than 20 percent of those submitted by experienced federal contractors are funded. Unsolicited submissions to any kind of foundation are even less successful.

For research grant proposals, respond only to specific proposal calls. And do so only after meeting and speaking in person to a point of contact in that organization to learn as much as possible about the research organization and their needs and goals.

Do not despair or give up if not successful. Get a debriefing from the organization when it is rejected. Call and request specific comments on the proposal—strengths and weaknesses. A federal agency is required to respond to your request for a debriefing. Use the various foundation directories described earlier to identify other organizations for which the proposal appears appropriate.

REFERENCES

Annual register of grant support, 1982–1983, 16th edition. (1982). Chicago: Marquis Professional Publications.

DRC: Directory of research grants. (1982). Phoenix, AZ: Oryx Press.

Government Information Services. (1980). *Guide to federal funding for governments and non-profits.* Arlington, VA: James J. Marshall.

Haile, S. W. (1991). *Foundation grants to individuals,* 7th edition. New York: Foundation Center.

Lewis, M. O., & Teitz-Gersumsky, A. (editors) (1981). *The foundation directory,* 8th edition. New York: The Foundation Center.

Luey, B. (1990). *Handbook for academic authors.* Cambridge, England: Cambridge University Press.

Meador, R. (1986). *Guidelines for preparing proposals.* Chelsea, MI: Lewis Publishers.

Publication grants for writers and publishers. (1991). Phoenix, AZ: Oryx Press.

Thomas, R. C., & Ruffner, J. A. (1982). *Research centers directory,* 7th edition. Detroit: Gale Research Company.

Chapter 8

Book Publication — Phase I: Pre-Contractual Considerations

Most academicians experience satisfaction, anticipation, and some anxiety when with their first signed publisher's contract in hand they begin to put together their first book. While at that point in time, an academic probably has written many published journal articles and conference papers, a book length work is much different. A book often demonstrates a greater level of academic achievement. It is also a more permanent contribution to one's field. It is usually built upon and a result of other works—journal articles, papers, and funded grant and/or other research findings which have been compiled. This is, in part, why this chapter follows the others.

The skills needed to develop a book manuscript successfully include many, if not all, of the abilities necessary to write journal articles, conference papers, and grant proposals. There are also other skills needed—such as identifying an appropriate publisher, writing a prospectus, marketing an idea, negotiating a contract, and writing and producing the manuscript. Finally, a writer needs to cooperate in marketing the book.

A THREE-PHASE APPROACH

The book writing process has three distinct phases (see Figure 8-1): (1) pre-contractual, (2) developmental, and (3) marketing. Pre-contractual considerations are described in this chapter; the other two phases are discussed in Chapters 9 to 11.

Figure 8-1
A Three-Phase Book Writing Process

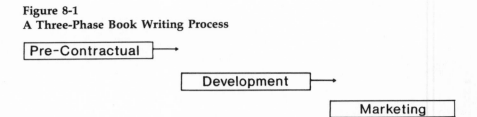

Pre-Contractual Considerations

Pre-contractual considerations begin as we think about our writing ideas and plans. Successful writers first deal with the book's topic. First clarify the subject matter you are planning to write about. Begin by developing a detailed outline; this helps to organize thoughts. If the work is based on past research and/or journal article writing, review the material—and keep it close by as a reference.

Write an outline for a manuscript prospectus in the form of a foreword or introduction aimed at the intended reader. This will help you to focus on the specific audience. Work back and forth between the table of contents or outline and the introductory section. Once satisfied with the topic and approach, identify a colleague in whom you have confidence and ask that person to review and critique the work. Discuss the ideas, topic, and treatment, and get a sense of how the material will be received by the intended audience and/or academic community.

It is important to be very familiar with the literature in the field. Conduct a literature search (see Chapter 3, Figure 3-1). The subject index in *Books in Print* is useful to discern such information. Obtain similar titles and review these works. Look for similarity to or differences from the intended work. Is there a unique niche, a specific area or approach, which will make a definite contribution to the field? Note the publishers of these existing books as they could very well be the first publishers to approach. Publishers tend to specialize in certain fields and subjects.

With a manuscript prospectus in hand, you are now ready to research potential publishers. This very important task is often underestimated by many academic writers. All too often colleagues asked why they are working with a particular publisher respond, "Because they agree to publish my book." This is not always the best way to make such a decision. It is better to focus on the kind of work one is developing or planning to develop. Establish some expectations of a potential publisher, and select a publisher that fulfills those objectives. Some specific characteristics of each category of publisher are described next.

Categories of Publishers

Generally speaking, there are three types of books—and publishers: (1) scholarly, (2) text, and (3) popular (or trade). Each of these looks for specific indicators when making a decision to contract a project. Therefore, formulate specific questions appropriate to the category of publisher.

Scholarly Publishers. Scholarly publishers concentrate on books which deal with specific topics and subjects in a research-based fashion. They are often developed and written with an approach analogous to that of a journal manuscript. These books generally are printed in relatively small quantities. There are several different organizational configurations for scholarly publishers: university presses, commercial scholarly publishers, university centers, and learned societies.

A scholarly publisher looks for a well-defined prospectus (book proposal) which shows evidence of significant primary data research. Several finished chapters, a bibliography, and a table of contents should also be prepared for review. The work also must fit the publisher's program. The credentials of the author(s) weigh heavily in a decision to publish. The author often "sells the work" in academic publishing. A refereed process is used by scholarly publishers, wherein the manuscript is read by several reviewers and the findings are then compiled and weighed by the publisher's editorial committee (Parsons, 1989).

University Presses. University presses are a principal source of publication of scholarly work—and were established just for that purpose. These presses are not-for-profit entities associated with colleges and universities. There are approximately one hundred such organizations in existence (Powell, 1985). *The Association of American University Presses Directory* includes information about each press. This is a very useful guide for preliminary information.

Academics and other professionals constitute a primary audience for scholarly publishers. However, the criteria used by scholarly publishers in their decision-making process vary. Although profit is not a primary element in selecting publishable material among university presses, fiscal factors have an impact. The scholarly nature of the work is ideally the primary variable; hence contribution to scholarship counts significantly.

There has been much controversy in the academic community about the "gatekeeping" role of the academic press. Mohr (1992) as well as others challenge the rationale for manuscript selection. Sales forecasts are necessary considerations, as are certain other factors, such as the following (Parsons, 1989, p. 123):

- work complements the press backlist
- author is a "respected name in the field"
- work has text potential

- author previously published a successful book(s)
- work promises to be controversial
- author is from a particularly selective institution

According to Mohr, "Academic freedom in the case of university presses means making decisions based on referees' reports. Reliance on these reports is the structural feature of university presses" (p. 44). Yet as Parson relates, academic presses have been actively developing a wide variety of specialized lists. An example of a title which expands upon a market for scholarly press is *The Colonial: The Life and Wars of Henry Stimson 1867–1950* by Godfrey Hodgson, a lucid and penetrating biography written for a popular audience published by a university press.

University presses concentrate their efforts in certain areas of specialization (list building), such as *Teacher's College Press*, educational and human services. Books such as Parsons (1989) and the *Directory of University Presses* describe university press lists and areas of concentration.

A university press often anticipates a run of no more than eight hundred to one thousand copies. Sometimes sales do not break even with costs. This causes some academic presses to seek subvention grants from authors. The author is asked to pay for part of the book's production costs, such as illustrations and copyright permissions, or to assure a level of purchase. Subventions are further discussed in Chapter 7.

University Centers. University centers are institutes with a specific scholarly mission. For instance, the Center for Community College Education at California State University, Los Angeles, has as its mission research and information dissemination for and about the community college. The center works with a commercial publisher to produce *New Horizons Series in Community College Education*; it also directly disseminates published information and works on grant subsidized publications. The ERIC Clearinghouse for Community College Education is also associated with the center. Another such publisher is associated with the National Academy of Science and the National Research Council. By collaborating with one or more of these centers, authors can often identify an opportunity to publish.

Learned Societies. Learned societies are also sources for publication of scholarly work. These are usually professional associations that sponsor a variety of professionally related activities including publication. The American Society for Training and Development (ASTD) and the National Society for Performance and Instruction (NSPI) are two learned societies which often publish monographs and other works.

Commercial Scholarly Presses. Commercial scholarly presses also consider sales markets in addition to scholarship when making a publishing decision. They need to see a basic return on investment before a positive publishing decision can be rendered. Commercial scholarly publishers may have a superior marketing and sales system—especially if the commercial scholarly press is a sub-division of a commercial trade publisher. These publishers focus on a well-developed academic market niche.

Commercial scholarly presses use many of the same criteria as university presses for selecting a work for publication. Usually a commercial scholarly press does not use a faculty committee per se but rather a referee-report system and draws upon a list of experienced academics who receive a honorarium for the completed review. Parsons (1989) suggests that commercial scholarly presses make faster decisions and offer shorter production cycles. A decision time line for review of a scholarly manuscript can be as long as or longer than that for a journal article but the author should ask the publisher to specify a schedule for decision.

Text Publishers. Text publishers are commercial houses that publish a general list of academic text and reference works. Text publishers look for a manuscript that has appeal to a specific audience and corresponding sales potential. Text publishing includes books for elementary and high school (EL-HI) instruction and college textbooks. Text publishing has gone through a great revolution over the last decade. Today text publishers, like any other kind of commercial entity, are cautious of high risks due to the rising costs of production and fierce competition. Many firms have been merged into larger publishing conglomerates. Much of the decision making has been centralized at higher corporate levels. A potential author needs to substantiate that the book has a definite market. Publishers often approach or commission established academics and offer attractive arrangements with them to facilitate text writing.

Text publishers cover a wide variety of products: college and EL-HI textbooks and associated materials (i.e., software, instructor guides, workbooks), reference books, paperback anthologies, and selected monographs. Some specialize in particular areas, such as business.

The larger text publishers tend to concentrate on books for traditional school and college courses; such books sell large numbers of copies if adopted by school districts or college programs. Smaller publishers tend to direct their efforts to more focused and specialized advanced courses. All publishers are, of course, listed in *Literary Marketplace*.

Authors in search of a publisher might browse the text catalogues that publishers mass-mail to colleges or universities. They can be located in individual college departments. Also, one might well search college bookstores for indications of a publisher's emphasis. In recent years, numerous titles and subjects aimed at the popular market have been published by scholarly and text publishers. Scholarly, text, and trade publishers alike reach out for a better educated and more well-informed general mass market.

Trade (Popular Book) Publishers. Publishers of popular or mass-market audience books, which include adult hardcover editions and paperbacks, are called trade publishers. Editors in scholarly and text houses usually seek outside expertise to assist in decision making, whereas trade book publishers usually rely on in-house guidance. Popular book publishing is high risk and ever changing. A sale of ten thousand to fifteen thousand copies is usually required to make a marginal profit, but a successful trade book can be very profitable. Popular book publishers attempt to stay abreast of cultural trends and consumer interest, with books such as Michael R. Beschloss and Edward Burlingame's (1992) *The Crisis Years: Kennedy and Khrushchev 1960–1963*, a dramatic scholarly account and analysis of a short but turbulent period in American history.

Popular publishing is not where most academics begin a publishing career. Nor is it the aim of this book to concentrate on this aspect of publishing. Yet, in recent years we have seen academics bridge the gap between scholarly and popular–mass market publishing. One success story is Depree's *Leadership Is an Art*, first published by a university press, and announced in *The Wall Street Journal*. Sandra Dijkstra (see Hall, 1991) recognized potential in the book and suggested that it be completely redone and the book was republished by a trade press. As of that article it had sold over 200,000 copies. In another instance, several professors of criminal justice produced very popular books on serial killer Ted Bundy, during and after his trial, while interest was high. Their work was an intellectual analysis of the events and circumstances. Very shortly after the death of the actor Michael Landon, a California college professor wrote a popular book on the actor's life. Sociologists and psychologists regularly transfer research into popular practice in topic areas such as history, political science, sex, marriage, and child rearing. Popular book publishing has appeal for those college professors who believe that they have material and ideas which can be broadly marketed. They should be aware that publishing in this market may not serve promotion or tenure purposes well. College faculty decision makers may not consider the effort or resulting work appropriate to the individual's academic role and responsibilities.

Vanity Press Publishing. Vanity presses are commercial entities that will "publish" and "distribute" a work for a fee. Vanity presses also look for works which appeal to a wider audience. Sometimes an author can get a publication into print with a vanity press by forgoing royalties. A vanity press agrees to design, produce, promote, and market a book in consideration of a publishing fee which offsets its expenses. The author assumes much of the risk for the book's ultimate success. In turn, the author can receive as much as 40 percent of the retail price of the book. This is a much better royalty than offered by text, trade, or scholarly book publishers. One should be aware that vanity publishing is not to be viewed as scholarly publishing by a university.

An alternative to a vanity press is self-publishing via electronic desktop publishing. The writer works as author, editor, printer, and distributor. More about this later.

Do Some Homework

Selecting a publisher is an important step. One should, clearly, seek to have options. If one plans a textbook, it is important to identify the market(s) to which the book will be directed. Successful textbook authors may give a publisher a representative list of institutions teaching courses that are directly related to the subject matter or approach. For those books that espouse a particular philosophy or practice, it is useful to provide references to other professors who also subscribe to that philosophy and who are likely to adopt the text. The publisher may welcome these references as potential technical reviewers of the manuscript. Be as specific as possible on numbers—potential markets, numbers of students, number of pages, graphics, and so forth. Publishers also need to know your schedule of development.

If a popular book is the choice, one should provide the sales analysis which will convince a publisher of the project's market appeal. This category of book is frequently marketed to publishers through an agent (Hall, 1991).

Large versus Small Publishers. Is a particular size of publishing house best for you? There are benefits and drawbacks to each. A large publishing house offers an author the benefits of name recognition and marketing prowess. The same well documented and written text may very well reach a wider audience through a large publisher than a smaller house. Part of this also has to do with the distribution and selling arrangements of a large publishing firm.

An author of a high potential work is often afforded significant publisher in-house technical support capabilities in the form of developmental editors, copy editors, designers, photo researchers, art professionals, and people to give assistance with special features. The benefits accruing to the publisher as a result of its experience and size can work to make an author, even a new author, a success.

On the downside, an author can expect to encounter more formality and levels of hierarchy in dealing with a large house; it may be difficult to reach true decision makers. The small publisher usually has a single person—maybe the firm's principal or only editor—working directly on a project with an author. Much decision making is done by this principal or editor and the author by phone or in person, without working through an elaborate chain of command. This shortens the period from the start of a project through getting into print for an author.

Other benefits accrue to an author working with a small firm. Small highly motivated publishers may spend more time and effort developing a personalized marketing plan for a new work. An author needs to weigh these pros and cons when seeking or choosing among publishers.

Developing a Book Prospectus or Proposal

Once plans have been developed to the point of knowing what you want to write about and for whom, it is important to ensure that a book proposal includes enough detail to describe fully how the research was conducted, what data will be included in the book, and how the topics will be treated. Describe the essential characteristics of the work. Provide a reason for a publisher to invest in it.

A prospectus includes a rationale for the effort, a table of contents, a resume or vita, and information about data sources. In addition, text publishers may require specific detail about why you are choosing to write your prospective book—what special approach (or idea or concept) you wish to pursue. Editors will want comparisons to already published work: the competition. You will also need to supply market information: Where will the book be directed? To whom? What schools or colleges? How many potential readers (students)? These kinds of details will weigh in the decision. The more potential readers the better.

The prospectus is at the center of the pre-contractual phase of the publishing process. Again, this is the document which describes to a publisher what and for whom an author intends to write.

Provide practical details of how the manuscript will be developed. Will it be typewritten or done on a word processor? What software will be used? Will a professional editor or editorial service be used in the preparation of the manuscript? Will the publisher be the principal editor? Will a disk copy of the manuscript be supplied? This may expedite the production of galleys of the book and ultimately save considerable costs in production of the book. Emphasize any graphic arts capability that is available if it is pertinent to the project.

MAKING INITIAL CONTACTS

When starting out to identify a publisher for a first book, do some homework in several areas. First, in the scholarly book arena, read *The Chronicle of Higher Education*. As mentioned in previous chapters, *The Chronicle* publishes information on new scholarly books in print each week. By looking at book topics and subjects and the particular presses publishing them, one will be able to see which press tends to specialize in a particular area. Specialty monograph presses are also periodically highlighted in *The Chronicle* in separate articles.

Another good source of information is the *Books in Print* series. Checking the new titles and subjects will reveal publishers appropriate to specific subjects. For trade (or popular) publisher references, *Writer's Digest*, *Writer's Market*, and *Literary Marketplace* are good sources, in addition to publishers' catalogues.

First Steps

Prior to mailing anything to a publisher, make a telephone call. Establish a specific editor contact at the house. This is absolutely essential for follow-up purposes. At this time one should determine whether the subject is at least of general interest to the editor and publisher. One will also better define specific prospectus requirements of the publisher. Very often, a representational chapter or two is required. This provides the publisher with insights as to an author's writing level, approach, and style. In any event, the phone call can establish whether the publisher has a potential interest in the project. It also provides a specific person to whom the materials can be addressed and a specific contact as the process continues.

Scholarly book publishers, just as in the case of journal articles, may favor the practice that permits submission of a prospectus to one publisher at a time. These publishers require a reasonable amount of time to render a decision. However, let a publisher know your projected schedule and when you can no longer wait. The same approach should be used with a textbook publisher. In the case of trade publishers, writers may wish to use an agent to facilitate the submission and scheduling process.

Literary Agents. Most trade publishers generally do not routinely deal directly with new authors; rather, they work through a literary agent. Hall (1991) says that more prestigious houses only work through an agent but periodically review some unsolicited manuscripts in search of a very small percentage which will make it to publication.

Good literary agents are well versed in the publishing industry and are familiar with key personnel. Agents are in a position to do manuscript screening and are able to identify publication potential. They may advise a writer about changes that need to be made before submission. Hit or miss submissions of a manuscript are costly—in terms of time (especially for a time-sensitive topic), cost (in a writer's time, as well as postage and reproduction expenses), and a writer's self-confidence as an author.

Seek the advice of an experienced, trusted colleague or friend when choosing to hire an agent. In the world of academe, one can locate a good reference—someone who works with an agent and can provide an introduction. A person who is familiar with the area of endeavor is in the best position to serve one's needs and interests.

The following section details information on contracts and negotiations, which are also part of the pre-contractual phase. The development phase of a project, including specifics of manuscript preparation, copyrights, graphics layout, software available, writing styles and hints, galley proofs, and seeing the project through to printing, is discussed in Chapter 9, along with the final phase of a project, marketing.

THE PUBLISHING CONTRACT

A first book publication is a milestone in an academic's life. The experience should be treated with the degree of care and seriousness that it deserves. A book's publication is a joint venture of a sort—between an author and a publisher. The author provides creative services, in terms of planning, research, conceptualization, writing, inputs for layout and marketing, and authority.

The publisher provides a range of services, including editing, graphics design, typesetting, printing, binding, warehousing, promotion, and marketing. It is important to conceptualize all of these factors in advance. In any event, as one can readily see, a mutually supportive partnership is needed.

A relationship commences with the signing of a publishing contract. The details of the roles and responsibilities of each party should be clearly stipulated. This is probably not an author's forté. Some of us may not be comfortable discussing or even debating such details as royalties, format, marketing, distribution, and rights. One may, of course, seek advice and consider retaining an attorney.

Many people who have published books have signed contracts without the advise of legal counsel. Yet some authors would not execute a contract without counsel's review. It is very important, of course, to be selective in one's choice of counsel. Publishing law is a specialized area. The circumstances requiring counsel are relatively vague and normally pertain only when large amounts of money are involved. If one exercises reasonable caution in reviewing the standard publisher's contract (Figure 8-2), a writer can do reasonably well without having a lawyer review the details. Of course, if money is not a concern, an attorney experienced in the field of publishing can read, review, explain, and perhaps amend the contract to your advantage.

If the work is a trade or popular book, where sales, distribution, and royalties are of paramount concern, a lawyer or agent specializing in publishing should be involved (Luey, 1990; Levine, 1988).

Some factors are important when making such decisions. First, what is the ultimate goal to be achieved by writing the book? Areas of importance relate to the motivation for writing in the first place. These are (or may be) the following:

1. A need to publish to prosper academically (probably the number one motivation in the academic world).

Figure 8-2
A Standard Publisher's Contract

AGREEMENT made this day of

between

(hereinafter referred to as the Publisher) and

who is a citizen of and whose address is

(hereinafter referred to as the Author).

It is understood that the word "Author," as used in this Agreement, and any reference to "Author" by the masculine singular pronoun, also means "Editor" or "Compiler" and includes all authors and/or editors or compilers, male or female, who are party to this Agreement, as well as his, her, or their heirs, executors, assigns and successors.

Grant of Book Publishing Rights

1. The Author grants to the Publisher and to its successors, representatives, divisions, imprints, affiliates and assigns, during the term of copyright, sole and exclusive right to publish or cause to be published in hardcover and/or paperbound book form under its own or other imprints in the English language in the United States of America and its dependencies and all other countries, including the right and license to print, manufacture, and sell, the Work now tentatively entitled (hereinafter referred to as the Work):

The Author also grants to the Publisher full, sole, and exclusive right to publish the Work in all other languages and countries throughout the world and to license the said Work for publication in all other languages and countries throughout the world during the term of the copyright of the Work.

Copyright

2. The Publisher will apply for all copyrights necessary to protect the Work in the United States and in such other countries as the Work can be copyrighted under the Universal Copyright Convention, in the name of the Author.

Delivery of Manuscript and Other Duties of Author

3. The Author agrees to deliver to the Publisher on or before , a complete ribbon copy and a clean duplicate of the Work in final and complete form judged acceptable and satisfactory by the Publisher as to both format and content. If the Author delivers only one copy of the manuscript of the Work, the Publisher will duplicate the manuscript for the Publisher's own use at the Author's expense. The Author will be billed for the cost of duplication, which cost is to be paid to the Publisher prior to acceptance of the Work. Except as may be provided elsewhere in this Agreement, the Work will contain a table of contents and a bibliography or a bibliographic essay, and the Author will be solely responsible for providing a general subject index, ready for production. If requested by the Publisher, the Author will also furnish at his own expense a preface or a foreword. The completed manuscript of the Work will be no more than

in length, inclusive of frontmatter; text; notes; bibliography or bibliographical essay; graphs, tables, charts, or other illustrations; and general subject index. In the event that an acceptable completed manuscript of the Work is more than ten percent (10%) longer than specified in Clause 3 of this Agreement, the Publisher will be free either to reduce the royalties specified in Sections A. and D. of this Clause 12 by one-half (1/2) or to require that the Author prepare the Work in camera-ready form according to specifications provided by the Publisher

Except as may be provided elsewhere in this Agreement, the Author is solely responsible for requesting and securing, as necessary or required, all final and complete copyright and other proprietary rights, licenses, permissions, or releases from the owners or holders of such rights, at no cost to the Publisher. The written evidence and record of all transactions, negotiations, and agreements concerning the requesting and receiving of all necessary and required permissions will be maintained in good order by the Author and transmitted, in complete form, to the Publisher at the time the Author submits the completed manuscript of the Work. Each written grant of permission will state the source of the material to be reprinted or reproduced, will cite

Figure 8-2 (continued)

a standard form of credit to the grantor of permission, and will specify the nonexclusive right to reprint, translate, reproduce, and publish the material throughout the world.

The Publisher will have the right to alter the manuscript to conform with the Publisher's standard style of capitalization, punctuation, spelling, and usage. The Author will maintain the checklist of manuscript style and elements and will transmit it in good order, in complete form, to the Publisher at the time the Author submits the completed manuscript of the Work.

Except as may be provided elsewhere in this Agreement, the Author is solely responsible for providing, at no cost to the Publisher, suitable camera-ready tables, graphs, diagrams, maps, photographs, and any other illustrations selected for inclusion, and approved by the Publisher.

Failure to Deliver Manuscript

4. If the Author fails to deliver the complete material as specified in Clause 3 within the specified time, the Publisher may extend the time in writing or terminate this Agreement and the Author will be obligated in the event of such termination to return any and all amounts which may have been advanced to the Author.

Proofreading; Additional Charge for AA's.

5. The Author agrees to read the copyedited manuscript of the Work if and as requested by the Publisher and to return the manuscript by first class mail insured within fifteen (15) days of receipt. Except as may be specifically provided elsewhere in this Agreement, the Author will make all necessary revisions in substance and in style prior to typesetting. The Author agrees to read the galley proofs of the Work, making only those revisions needed to correct printer's errors and to correct errors in fact and to update the Work as requested by the Publisher, and to return the proofs by first class mail insured within fifteen (15) days of receipt. The Author agrees to read page proofs, to finalize the index, noted in Clause 3, and to return the material to the Publisher by first class mail insured within ten (10) days of receipt unless specified otherwise by the Publisher. The Author will pay the costs incurred by the Publisher because of changes and/or additions made by the author on proofs (Author's Alterations or AA's), other than corrections of printer's errors. This cost will be billed directly to the Author or deducted from the Author's royalties and earnings on the sale of the Work as determined by the Publisher.

Manner of Publication

6. All decisions and details as to the publication of the Work, including style, illustrations, time and manner of production, price, advertisement and the number and distribution of free copies will be left to the sole discretion of the Publisher, who will bear all expenses of production, publication, and advertisement.

Revised or Subsequent Editions

7. The Author agrees to revise the first and subsequent editions of the Work at the request of the Publisher and to supply any new matter necessary from time to time to keep the Work up to date. If the Author shall neglect or be unable to revise or supply new matter, the Publisher may engage some other person or persons to revise or to supply such new matter and may deduct the expenses thereof from royalties accruing to the Author on such revised subsequent editions. It is understood that if such revisions are made by someone other than the Author, the Publisher will cause such fact to be evident in the revised subsequent edition. The Publisher will have all of the rights in connection with all subsequent editions that it is entitled to in the original Work.

Option for Next Work

8. The Author grants to the Publisher the exclusive option to publish his next substantial work. The Publisher shall be entitled to a period of sixty (60) days after the submission of the completed manuscript in which to notify the Author in writing whether it desires to publish such manuscript.

Author's Warranty and Indemnification

9. The Author represents and warrants that he is the sole author and proprietor of the Work and that he has the full power to make this Agreement and grant, that it in no way infringes upon any copyright or proprietary right of others, and that it contains nothing unlawful, libelous, or in violation of any right of privacy. The Author will indemnify and hold harmless the Publisher from any and all liability, expenses, or damages arising out of the contents of the Work or the Author's performance of his duties under this Agreement, including, without limitation, libel, plagiarism, copyright infringement or the publication of unlawful matter, except with respect to any matter added upon request of the Publisher. Said indemnity will extend to and include the fees of counsel selected by the Publisher and other expenses incurred by the Publisher in the defense of any claim, even though the claim may not be finally sustained. Publisher agrees to notify the Author promptly upon the receipt of any claim. The Author agrees to cooperate fully with the Publisher in the defense of such claim.

Noncompetition

10. The Author further warrants and agrees that he will not during the full term of this Agreement furnish to any other publisher any work on the same subject directly competitive with the Work covered by this Agreement.

Grant of Other Rights

11. The Author hereby grants to the Publisher during the full term of the copyright of the Work and all renewals thereof the following sole and exclusive rights in all languages and in all countries: abridgement, condensation, digest, syndication, and serial rights; book club rights and the right to publish the Work or

Figure 8-2 (continued)

cause or permit its publication with others in a set or sets in an omnibus volume with other works and in cheap or reprint edition or editions, and the right to make or cause, or permit the making, of mechanical renditions and/or recordings of the Work or any part or parts thereof, in visualized or sound form, singly or in a combination or partly in each; the television, radio broadcasting, dramatic, motion picture, and microform rights; and the rights for all other non-printed and electronically produced or reproduced versions.

Royalty Schedule

12. A. REGULAR CLOTHBOUND EDITION: on all sales of the Work, less returns, in the United States and its territories and dependencies, on the net price of the Work (actual cash received), except as hereinafter provided, the Author will receive a total royalty of

One-half (1/2) of the foregoing royalty(ies) will be paid on all sales, less returns, made outside the United States and its dependencies and territories.

B. HIGH DISCOUNT SALE: on copies sold at a special discount of sixty percent (60%) or more from the retail price of the Publisher's edition of the Work or an edition of the Work manufactured by the Publisher for an imprint other than the Publisher's, the Publisher will pay the Author a flat royalty of ten percent (10%) of the amount of the Publisher's receipts from sales, less returns, unless sold at or below manufacturing cost, in which case there will be no royalty paid. One-half (1/2) of the foregoing royalty(ies) will be paid on all sales, less returns, made outside the United States and its dependencies and territories.

C. SALE OF SHEETS: on all sales of sheets (unbound books) the Publisher will pay the Author a flat royalty of ten percent (10%) of the amount of the Publisher's receipts from sales, less returns, unless sold at or below the Publisher's cost, in which case there will be no royalty paid. One-half (1/2) of the foregoing royalty(ies) will be paid on all sales, less returns, made outside the United States and its dependencies and territories.

D. CHEAP OR PAPERBOUND EDITION BY PUBLISHER: if the Publisher publishes its own cheap or paperbound edition, it will pay to the Author a royalty of five percent (5%) of the net price for all copies sold of the edition, less returns. One-half (1/2) of the foregoing royalty(ies) will be paid on all sales, less returns, made outside the United States or its dependencies and territories.

E. CHEAP OR PAPERBOUND EDITION BY ANOTHER PUBLISHER: if the Publisher licenses the publication of a cheap or paperbound edition of the Work to another publisher, the Author will receive one-half (1/2) of the royalties or licensing income paid to the Publisher.

F. BOOK CLUBS: if the Publisher grants a book club the right to manufacture and publish the Work, it will pay the Author one-half (1/2) of the royalties or fees paid to it by the book club. If the Publisher grants a book club the right to distribute a Publisher's supplied edition of the Work, the Publisher will pay the Author one-half (1/2) of the amount of the Publisher's receipts from such a sale, after the costs of manufacturing and supplying the book club edition have been deducted from such receipts.

G. CONSUMER SALES: on copies sold by the Publisher direct to individual consumers through mass-market coupon advertising, radio or television advertising, and house-to-house solicitation, the Publisher will pay the Author one-half (1/2) of the royalty(ies) stipulated in section A. of Clause 12.

H. TRANSLATION RIGHTS AND FOREIGN LANGUAGE EDITIONS: if the Publisher licenses the publication of foreign language editions of the Work, the Publisher will pay the Author one-half (1/2) of the licensing fee or royalty(ies) paid to the Publisher.
On any foreign language edition of the Work prepared by the Publisher, the Publisher will pay the Author one-half (1/2) of the royalty(ies) stipulated in section A. of Clause 12. If the Author makes his own translation, or arranges for and secures a translation at no cost to the Publisher, the Author will receive the royalty(ies) stipulated in section A. of Clause 12, on all sales, less returns, made by the Publisher of the Work in translation.

I. NO ROYALTY COPIES: on copies furnished free to the Author or purchased by the Author at the Author's discount and on copies furnished to others for review, advertising, sample or like purpose, no royalties will be paid.

J. SUBSIDIARY INCOME: the Publisher will pay the Author one-half (1/2) of the Publisher's receipts from the licensing of the following rights: abridgement, condensation, digest, syndication, and anthologizing of the Work; the Publisher will pay the Author ten percent (10%) of any licensing income derived from the making of mechanical renditions, recordings in visualized or sound form, television, radio, dramatic, motion picture, microform and other non-printed and electronically produced or reproduced versions. If the Publisher itself should produce, publish or issue the Work in any form listed above in section J., the Author will receive royalties as stipulated in section A. of Clause 12 on sales of the Work in such version.

Figure 8-2 (continued)

Information about the Author	13. The Author agrees to submit a completed Author's Questionnaire on or before submission of the manuscript of the Work and to permit the Publisher to use his name and affiliations, and publicly available facts about the Author's education, employment, professional affiliations, and publications in advertising and promotional material related to the Publisher's business and to the Work. The Publisher agrees to use all such information relating to the Author in a reasonable and ethical manner.
Royalty Statements	14. The Publisher will submit to the Author annual royalty statements between October first (1st) and December first (1st) of each year for the annual period ending the previous June thirtieth (30th). Whenever the annual sales fall below twenty-five (25) copies, no accounting will be made until the end of the annual period in which aggregate sales will have reached twenty-five (25) copies.
Author's Copies	15. The Publisher will provide the Author with five (5) free copies of the first edition of the Work and with one (1) free copy of any other edition of the Work published by the Publisher. The Author will have the right to purchase up to twenty-five (25) copies of the Work for his own use, and not for resale, charging said copies against royalties at a discount of forty percent (40%) from the retail price, provided said order is submitted before or at the time of publication of the Work. Following publication of the Work, the Author may purchase copies of the Work, in any quantity, for his own use and not for resale, at a discount of forty percent (40%) from the retail price, provided such orders are accompanied by prepayment (check or credit card). No royalties will be paid to the Author on the sales specified in Clause 15. Also, as a courtesy, the Author will have the right to purchase any other books published by the Publisher at a thirty percent (30%) discount from the retail price, plus shipping and handling. Books purchased at this special discount are for the Author's own use, and not for resale, and orders are limited to single copies only. Such orders must be clearly marked "Author's Courtesy Discount" and must be accompanied by prepayment.
Author's Property	16. The Publisher will not be responsible for loss or damage to any property of the Author in its possession or that of any independent contractors, or in possession of anyone else to whom delivery is made by the Publisher.
Sums Due and Owing	17. Any sums due and owing from the Author to the Publisher will be forthwith charged to and paid by the Author and may be deducted from any sums due to or to become due from the Publisher to the Author, whether by reason of this Agreement or any other agreement between the parties.
Application of Laws	18. This Agreement will be interpreted according to the laws and statutes of the State of Connecticut and of the United States of America, regardless of the place of its physical execution.
Modification	19. This Agreement constitutes the complete understanding of the parties and no representation other than is contained herein will be binding. No alteration, modification, or waiver of any provision hereof will be valid unless in writing and signed by both parties.
Assignment of Obligations	20. The Author may not assign his obligations under this Agreement without the written consent of the Publisher.

Agreed to and Accepted:

For and on behalf of
Inc.:

By _____

_____

AUTHOR

Soc. Sec. No. _____

Date _____   Date _____

2. A desire to add knowledge to a discipline, theory, or concept. Hence as a writer you have an important story to tell.
3. A need to establish yourself as an expert in the field.
4. A desire to profit from writing.

If the motivation is for the most part academic, royalties probably are of less importance. Likewise, the other fiduciary areas of the contract also are of little or no immediate interest. Writers may wish to attempt to negotiate an advance against anticipated royalties. This provides some working capital. A potential tactic would be to negotiate for half of the expected royalties for the first year, on a non-returnable basis. The publisher would, of course, have to perceive a competitive situation and significant market potential to agree.

Taking a closer look at a standard publisher's contract is the next task. Each major clause in Figure 8-2 is discussed in the following sections. It is called a standard contract because most of the language and clauses are incorporated in all publishing contracts. One can attempt to negotiate most language in a contract (Levine, 1988).

Grant of Book Publishing Rights

The first set of paragraphs of a standard publishing contract is called *Grant of Book Publishing Rights* (or *Author's Grant*). The contract opens with the names of the parties bound by the agreement. In these paragraphs, an author grants or agrees to give the publisher full, sole, and exclusive right to publish the work, whose complete title is spelled out. These paragraphs usually contain language conveying the rights to all possible versions of the work: paperback, hardbound, in all languages, in all countries where the book is sold, and the like. Note the following language, taken from a typical publisher's contract:

The Author grants to the Publisher and to its successors, representatives, divisions, imprints, affiliates and assigns, during the term of copyright, sole and exclusive right to publish or cause to be published in hardcover and/or paperbound book form under its own or other imprints in the English language in the United States of America and its dependencies and in all other languages and countries throughout the world, including the right and license to print, manufacture, and sell, the Work now tentatively entitled (hereinafter referred to as the Work):

[Title inserted here]

during the term of the copyright of the Work.

Yes, the right to print in *all other* languages is also conveyed to the publisher! Often English-language rights to print in countries such as Great

Britain, Australia, Canada, New Zealand, and South Africa are reserved
by the author, or otherwise protected, as such rights become valuable for
a strongly selling book. Be as specific as possible in conveying such rights.
An author may wish to have the rights to some of these options revert
to him or her after two to five years if the publisher has been unsuccessful
in marketing the work to other countries or in other forms after the period
has elapsed. A clause such as the following might be advisable (Levine,
1988, p. 4–6): "All rights in the Work not specifically licensed herein to
the Publisher are reserved to the Author."

Delivery of Manuscript

The next paragraphs specify the conditions and date for delivery of the
manuscript. An author usually agrees to deliver to the publisher, on or
before an agreed upon date, a complete copy of the work in final and
complete form and in a specified format. The publisher usually reserves
the right to judge what is acceptable and satisfactory. The work contains
a table of contents and a bibliography or a bibliographic essay, and the
author is usually responsible for providing a general subject index, ready
for production. Preparation of indexes can be negotiated. Writers often
request either financial or consultant support to do indexes. A writer can
also negotiate the number of double-spaced pages (manuscript length),
including frontmatter, text, notes, bibliographical essay, graphs, tables,
charts, or other illustrations; and general subject index. Publishers are
concerned with excessively long manuscripts. Therefore, language such
as the following is not uncommon:

In the event that an acceptable completed manuscript of the Work is more than
ten percent (10%) longer than specified in this Agreement, the Publisher will be
free either to reduce the royalties specified in this contract or to require that the
Author prepare the Work in camera-ready form according to specifications
provided by the Publisher.

Permissions

Authors are also responsible for securing copyright releases and
permission for use of material which they quote or reproduce from others.
An author usually has a legal obligation to protect the publisher from
disagreements or lawsuits arising out of copyright disputes brought by
others for infringements claimed against a writer and his or her work.
Clauses to look for in a contract include the following:

With the manuscript the Author shall deliver written permissions satisfactory to
the Publisher in all editions of the Work of any graphic or textual material from

published or unpublished works of others, including any permissions required for any additional materials.

Copyright releases and permissions can be expensive. Permission to reprint a single figure can cost fifty dollars and up for English-language rights for a single printing only. If large numbers of copyright releases from other works are anticipated, a writer may wish to negotiate a share-cost arrangement with the publisher. Authors must also provide written grant of permission stating the source of the material to be reprinted or reproduced, with a standard form of credit to the grantor of permission, specifying the non-exclusive right to reprint, translate, reproduce, and publish the material throughout the world.

Standard contracts provide that authors will assume responsibility for preparing or securing camera-ready tables, charts, and graphics for inclusion in the text. The cost and intricacies of preparation of graphics are often overlooked by new authors. Publishers often charge authors for special requirements which exceed the contractual limits. Notice the following typical clause. Be sure to estimate your needs correctly ahead of time.

Except as may be provided elsewhere in this Agreement, the Author is solely responsible for providing, at no cost to the Publisher, suitable camera-ready tables, graphs, diagrams, maps, photographs, and any other illustrations selected for inclusion, and approved by the Publisher.

Be sure that the editorial and copy preparation support to be provided are understood and what, if any, additional support will be required.

Give attention to the conditions under which the book cover, jacket, and promotional copy will be designed and developed. Take note of the applicable contract clauses.

Failure to Deliver Manuscript. If a writer fails to meet the stipulated deadline, the standard contract allows the publisher the option of terminating the contract or extending the deadline. Undoubtedly, this decision would be made after looking at what progress has been made toward completion. If any money has been advanced, one may be obligated to repay it. Think about the publisher's turn-around time and deadline. Make sure deadlines are set for publisher responsibilities as well. For instance, a typical "failure to deliver manuscript" clause follows:

If the Author fails to deliver the complete material as specified within the specified time, the Publisher may extend the time in writing or terminate this Agreement and the Author will be obligated in the event of such termination to return any and all amounts which may have been advanced to the Author.

And what if the publisher fails to get the work into print? Contract language which protects the author in this circumstance such as the following (also see Levine, 1988) is desirable:

Upon receipt of the original Work, the Publisher will review and edit same, and provide feedback to the Author in written form within 90 working days.

Should a manuscript be unacceptable to the publisher, the author should be notified within a specified period, with a list of specific areas in which the manuscript is deficient.

The publisher may also agree to publish the work within a given period after receipt of the completed manuscript. Should the publisher fail to publish in accordance with the contract provisions (and some should be made), all rights (including copyright) shall, at the author's option, revert to the author.

Copyright Protection

A publisher has an obligation to protect a book by copyright. Contract language which should be present follows:

The Publisher will apply for all copyrights necessary to protect the Work in the United States and in such other countries as the Work can be copyrighted under the Universal Copyright Convention, in the name of the Author. Copyright in the Work shall remain the property of the Author. The Publisher agrees to take steps necessary to ensure protection of the copyright, including the placing of a copyright notice in the name of the Author sufficient to protect the Author's rights in every copy published or licensed.

Proofreading and Manner of Publication

Review of and response to copyedited materials and reading of proofs are a writer's responsibilities. The terms should always be spelled out in the contract. Often to protect the publisher from last-minute changes, the publisher inserts language in the contract which would assign a cost (in royalties) to an author who demanded changes at the proof stage of production. The publisher wants to reserve the right to decide on the appearance of the book, its retail price, who will receive complimentary copies, how it will be advertised, and how it will be promoted. These are the areas in which much negotiation is often done on more popular (trade) works, and where attorneys often become involved. The contract should stipulate that the publisher will assume *all* costs for publication, advertising, and distribution.

The Publisher will have the right to alter the manuscript to conform with the Publisher's standard style of capitalization, punctuation, spelling, and usage. The Author will maintain the checklist of manuscript style and elements and will transmit it in good order, in complete form, to the Publisher at the time the Author submits the completed manuscript of the Work.

Revised or Subsequent Editions

The next series of paragraphs (discussed later) should be studied carefully. They require that an author will make revisions, update, and/or change the work at the discretion of the publisher in order to keep the book up-to-date. This binds authors to the work for as long as the publisher wishes to keep the title active. If one loses interest in the work or otherwise does not wish to comply, the publisher may select someone to replace the author, assign credits to the new person, and redirect the royalties to the revisor.

A typical clause states:

The Author agrees to revise the first and subsequent editions of the Work at the request of the Publisher and to supply any new matter necessary from time to time to keep the work up to date. If the Author shall neglect or be unable to revise or supply new matter, the Publisher may engage some other person or persons to revise or to supply such new matter and may deduct the expenses thereof from royalties accruing to the Author on such revised subsequent editions. It is understood that if such revisions are made by someone other than the Author, the Publisher will cause such fact to be evident in the revised subsequent edition. The Publisher will have all of the rights in connection with all subsequent editions that it is entitled to in the original Work.

The best arrangement to aim for is a statement that no changes to the work are permitted without the consent of both author and publisher.

Representations and Warranties

The next paragraph stipulates that the author(s) own(s) the rights to the manuscript under contract—and has the exclusive right to offer it for publication. This is an extension of the copyright issue discussed earlier.

The Author represents and warrants that he is the sole author and proprietor of the Work and that he has the full power to make this Agreement and grant, that it in no way infringes upon any copyright or proprietary right of others, and that it contains nothing unlawful, libelous, or in violation of any right of privacy. The Author will indemnify and hold harmless the Publisher from any and all liability, expenses, or damages arising out of the contents of the Work or the Author's performance of his duties under this Agreement, including, without limitations, libel, plagiarism, copyright infringement or the publication of unlawful matter, except with respect to any matter added upon request of the Publisher. Said indemnity will extend to and include the fees of counsel selected by the Publisher and other expenses incurred by the Publisher in the defense of any claim, even though the claim may not be finally sustained. Publisher agrees to notify the Author promptly upon the receipt of any claim. The Author agrees to cooperate fully with the Publisher in the defense of such claim.

Be careful to ensure that as author(s) one has full rights to the work. Some related issues are discussed in Chapter 9 under the topic of intellectual property and copyright.

Royalties

What will an author actually get for all of this? Next is the royalty schedule. The schedule begins with sales of regular clothbound editions—the standard. In scholarly publishing, it usually describes royalties in terms of "net price of the book": the cash actually received by the publisher. It then discusses royalties for other than regular sales, which includes high discount sales, paperbound editions, paperbound editions by another publisher, book clubs, consumer sales (mass market advertising), foreign editions, and subsidiary rights. Generally speaking, royalties on scholarly works are stipulated as a percentage of net sales (the price of the book sold to the bookstore or wholesale distributor). Tradebooks pay royalties based on percentage of list price (the over the counter price). Textbooks usually pay royalties between 10 and 15 percent of net, whereas trade books usually begin at 6 percent list (with an ascending scale for above ten thousand copies sold). A typical author's royalty rate for a college text ranges from 10 to 18.75 percent of the publisher's net receipts (equal to sales minus returns). The royalty schedule for scholarly books is usually much less and is based on net sales (6 to 9 percent). Perhaps an accountant would be helpful in interpreting this part of the contract. The contract also provides for an author to receive a statement of royalties and payment of amounts due once or twice a year.

An author should also provide for rights to accounting. Specifically, look for language such as this.

(a) After publication, the Publisher will render statements annually to the Author during the month of April for the preceding period January to December. Each statement will be accompanied by payment to the Author of the amount shown to be due on the statement, after a reasonable reserve for returns. If less than $25.00 is due for any accounting period, the Publisher may render no statement or payment until after the year in which more than $25.00 is due the Author.

The Author or Author's representative shall be entitled to inspect the Publisher's accounting records with respect to sales of the Work.

and

The Publisher will submit to the Author annual royalty statements between October first (1st) of each year for the annual period ending the previous June thirtieth (30th). Whenever the annual sales fall below twenty-five (25) copies, no accounting will be made until the end of the annual period in which aggregate sales will have reached twenty-five (25) copies.

Free Copies. Author copies become of interest as soon as a book becomes reality. It may be too late to negotiate free copies at that point, although one can always make a case for additional copies. Authors should negotiate for the number of copies desired from the publisher at the time of signing the contract. This is usually an area where publishers give a little.

Option for Next Work

The next paragraph binds an author to a publisher on a right-of-first-refusal basis for a next substantial manuscript. This can limit a writer's ability to market himself or herself to the fullest potential, if one feels another publisher is more suitable for a next work.

The Author grants to the Publisher the exclusive option to publish his next substantial work. The Publisher shall be entitled to a period of sixty (60) days after the submission of the completed manuscript in which to notify the Author in writing whether it desires to publish such manuscript.

Of course, an author can request higher royalties than the publisher can afford to pay in order to force the publisher to decline the right to publish the manuscript. However, the best course of action is not to agree to such a clause.

Non-Competition Relationship with Other Contracts

The following paragraph limits the ability to develop any future work for any other publisher which may compete with this work. Relate this thought to the paragraph on "the option for next work." A typical clause in a contract to protect a publisher against book competition is the following:

The Author further warrants and agrees that he will not during the full term of this Agreement furnish to any other publisher any work on the same subject directly competitive with the Work covered by this Agreement.

Directly is the key word here. As long as one is not planning on writing several works of essentially the same nature, this should not be a problem. However, an author who does plan to publish even similar work for other audiences should discuss this with the publisher.

Termination

Once the work goes out of print or the publisher ceases to exist, an author needs to protect the manuscript's property rights. "Reversion of rights" clauses read as follows:

The Author may terminate this agreement by written notice to the Publisher in the following instances: All rights in the Work shall then, at the option of the Author, revert to the Author.
(a) Failure to Publish: if the Publisher fails to publish the Work within the agreed period;
(b) Work Out of Print: if following publication the Publisher fails to report any sales of the work for any period of 12 months, or does not make the book available for sale in any edition of the Publisher or its licensees and refuses to reissue the Work within 6 months after written demand from the Author; or
(c) Defaults in Payment: if the Publisher fails to pay any monies owing when due for a period of three months after written demand from the Author.

Subsidiaries

The Author will be entitled to one-half of the proceeds received by the Publisher under any license granted by the Publisher under the provisions of this clause.
(a) Hardcover and paperback reprint editions; book club; anthology; abridgement, condensation, digest, and selection (textual, graphic, and other materials); filmstrip (whether or not synchronized with sound); transparency; microfilm; programmed instruction, computer program, information storage and retrieval, and all other non-book forms of reproduction, now or hereafter known, intended to display or otherwise make the Work or parts thereof available for reading; sound recording, audiovisual, television, and motion-picture versions, by any method now or hereafter known; all performance rights; rights to prepare and publish derivative works in any form or medium.

Such clauses should be negotiated in light of the specific project's potential.

Other Clauses

The last point to be made with respect to contracts has to do with special clauses which are emerging as a result of rising production costs of publishing. Some contracts specify the delivery of a camera-ready manuscript.

This means in essence that authors have the sole responsibility of supplying material in a form ready for printing. All page layouts, graphics cutting, heads, and the like, are the author's responsibility. This constitutes the bulk of the work in preparing a book for production. Some contracts have language as follows:

Editing the Manuscript
The Publisher may edit the manuscript in accordance with its standard style of capitalization, punctuation, spelling, and usage. The Publisher and the Author will mutually agree on the title of the Work.

Corrections of Proof
The Publisher shall submit one or more sets of galley or page proofs to the Author and allow the Author a reasonable time in which to make corrections. The Author will promptly read, correct, and return these proofs to the Publisher. The Publisher will be responsible for the cost of all changes made by the Author in the original set of proofs (which may be page proofs, galley proofs or copy edited manuscript). The Author will be responsible for the cost of changes made by the Author (excluding corrections of compositor's errors) in any subsequent proofs, and the excess costs will be deductible from amounts due to the Author. If, for any reason, after the proof has been submitted to the Author, the Author fails to return proof within the time set by the Publisher, the Publisher may make corrections it deems necessary and may proceed to publish the Work without benefit of the Author's corrections.

Design of Work
The Publisher shall retain the final decision on all matters relating to the appearance of the book. The name of the Author shall appear with due prominence on the title page, spine and dust-jacket or cover of every copy of the Work and in all advertising of the Work issued by the Publisher, its licensees or its agents.

Advertising and Promotion

Finally, what about marketing? Here is typical language to look for:

(a) The Publisher shall use its best efforts to promote, advertise and distribute the Work in order to sell the Author's Work to as many readers as possible, and shall consult with the Author on matters relating to the advertising and promotion of the Work.
(b) The Author authorizes use of the Author's name and picture for purposes of advertising and promotion in connection with the Work.

REFERENCES

The Association of American University Presses directory, 1990–1991. (1990). New York: Association of American University Presses.
Beschloss, M. R., & Burlingame, E. (1992). *The crisis years: Kennedy and Krushchev 1960–1963.* New York: Harper Perennial.

Center for Community College Education. (1987). *New horizons series in community college education*. Los Angeles: California State University at Los Angeles.

Chronicle of Higher Education (1991). New scholarly books in print. Washington, D.C.

Hall, K. (1991). The publishing journey. *Training & Development Journal*, August, 31–38.

Hodgson, G. (1992). *The colonial: The life and wars of Henry Stimson 1867–1950*. Chicago: Northwestern University Press.

Levine, M. L. (1988). *Negotiating a book contract. A guide for authors, agents and lawyers*. Mt. Kisco, NY: Moyer Bell Limited.

Literary marketplace: The directory of the American book publishing industry (1991). New York: R. R. Bowker.

Luey, B. (1990). *Handbook for academic authors*. Cambridge, England: Cambridge University Press.

Mohr, R. D. (1992). Point of view: When university presses give in to bias, academic principle will be disregarded. *The Chronicle of Higher Education*, July 15, A-44.

Neff, G. T. (editor). (1990). *1990 writer's market: Where & how to sell what you write*. Cincinnati: Writer's Digest Books.

Parsons, P. (1989). *Getting published: The acquisition process at university presses*. Knoxville: The University of Tennessee Press.

Powell, W. W. (1985). *Getting into print: The decision-making process in scholarly publishing*. Chicago: University of Chicago Press.

Chapter 9

Book Publication – Phase II: Developmental Considerations for Scholarly Books and College Texts

This chapter looks at writing both scholarly books and college texts. Scholarly book publishing is perhaps the single-most sought after academic accomplishment—especially in the early years of an academic appointment. Tenure and promotion committees view the scholarly book as prime evidence of academic accomplishment. A scholarly book, like an academic journal article, is refereed. A panel of experts have usually made a blind review and the publisher has deemed the manuscript worthy of publication.

Think critically about scholarly book publishing. To develop a book prospectus one needs to have a perspective or message to communicate. Many of the same rules apply to scholarly book publishing as to journal article publishing. Scholars who have been developing a line of inquiry via publishing journal articles and, perhaps, invited conference papers may very well have established a data base or empirical foundation for either a scholarly book or a college text manuscript.

DECIDING ON A PUBLISHER

As discussed in Chapter 3, it is important for the prospective writer of an academic book to research publishers before preparing and submitting a prospectus and book plan. Consider the publisher's reputation in the field. Some information can be gained through personal observation of books from various publishers. Consider the quality of the product in terms of design, production, and of course marketing prowess. Again, familiarize yourself with various sources of information about publishers (see Chapters 3 and 8).

DEVELOPING A BOOK PROSPECTUS

Whether you are developing a scholarly work or a college text, certain elements of a prospectus should be researched, developed, and written:

1. A cover letter providing a concise description of the proposed work. Highlight the special niche, features, or approach and the targeted audience. Describe the market competition, including other books, publications, and approaches taken. Discuss the state of development or anticipated schedule of completion and the additional resources required if any. Note that scholarly presses generally welcome essentially complete works; text publishers prefer to be able to "mold the work" and prefer a well developed idea, but not a completed manuscript. Also include information about the manuscript's characteristics such as length, illustrations, tables, and appendices. Editors like to know whether authors have the ability to submit the work in an electronic (disk) format, and whether authors can do their own illustration artwork.

2. Include a detailed table of contents. The more complete it appears, the more likely the editor will see potential in the work and be able to render an appropriate, informed decision.

3. Include a preface to introduce the work and its purpose. Use the kind of language which will be used throughout the work. The preface should convince the reader that the book has specific value. Likewise, it should convince the editor of the book's worth.

4. For a scholarly book include two or three sample chapters.

5. For a college text you may include a sample chapter to acquaint the editor with your writing style. It is particularly important to address the approach or characteristics which distinguish the proposed text from those now successful in the market. Why will it succeed? Generally speaking, college text editors would prefer not to have to handle more than one chapter while making the initial decision. The college text is normally more of a collaborative process involving the publisher, editor, reviewers, and author.

6. A complete author (and co-author) resume or vita should be included with the prospectus. Provide information and evidence of the writer's (s') qualifications to write the book, and recognition as (an) expert(s) in the proposed field for eventual marketing purposes of the book.

With this information in hand the editor can begin the review process.

MANUSCRIPT PROSPECTUS REVIEW PROCESSES

For a scholarly work, a prospectus review is often much like a refereed journal article review. It is sent out to a panel of referees, who work with the scholarly press on such decisions. The time used in this process is generally less than six months. Writers receive a communication from the editor informing them of any interest and whether revisions are suggested pending a second round review leading to a final decision. The latter is much like a conditional acceptance of a journal article. One should discuss with the editor the likelihood of an acceptance after making the suggested revisions, because considerable work and numerous changes may be required to suit the publisher's specification(s).

The college text decision process is different. Often the book proposal decision is made by a committee of in-house editors. An initial screening by an acquisitions editor identifies proposals which meet the house's publishing priorities. Market factors, approach, writing style, author qualifications, and overall suitability are considered. If the proposal meets preliminary screening benchmarks, it receives further consideration.

Often the editorial committee decides to submit the table of contents and sample chapter(s) to outside reader-consultants for comment. In small publishing houses a single editor/principal may make a decision—or may use an external consultant reviewer who is a regular consultant.

Authors who want options or choices may wish to submit the work to two or more publishers simultaneously. However, in a cover letter provide a time frame to the publisher, indicating that you have done so and a date when you must have a response. If the publisher expresses interest, negotiation is still required (see Chapter 8).

DEVELOPING THE WORK—A POINT OF COMMENCEMENT

Working with Your Publisher

A book publication is a team effort involving you and a publisher. Sometimes, in the case of a small publishing house, your teammate may be one editor. Or in large companies there may be specialists including developmental and copy editors, production coordinators, artists and layout people, and marketing coordinators involved. At the outset of a project an author needs to learn about the publisher's staff, their roles, mutual expectations, and available support.

A larger publisher may commence a publication project with a launch meeting. Each of the staff people who will be involved meets with an author to plan aspects of the project. Topics which need to be discussed include the schedule review process and the work's format. Electronic manuscript production is also discussed at this meeting.

Scholarly monographs are usually edited after the entire project is submitted. Textbook projects usually require chapters to be reviewed as they are developed so that project editors can monitor progress and development, and shape and guide the overall text development. The editor's objective is not to usurp a writer's role but rather to assist in producing a marketable product. The early chapter edits serve as a focal point for the overall writing style. Issues of writing style, tone, format, and perhaps chapter ordering surface during initial chapter edits. Text projects receive detailed editorial attention because they must read well and be accurate in every detail.

The initial meeting may also include discussion of marketing strategies and academic focus for the book. Ancillary products such as workbooks, computer software for exercises, study guides, and teacher's manuals are discussed if the text requires them in order to be successfully marketed. Give some preliminary thought to these, as you may very well be asked either to produce them yourself or to recommend someone else to do so.

Marketing specialists will want to identify the best way to plan preliminary marketing of the product and will develop a marketing strategy for the book once it is ready to be distributed. Authors should think about applicable media (journals, magazines, conferences) and about mailing lists which can be acquired (more about this in Chapter 11).

Either at the preliminary meeting or at a future time you will need to discuss the process for both content reviews and editorial reviews, both of which are necessary for textbook success. Issues of publisher's artwork staff support for illustrations, photographs, or charts also need to be discussed; textbooks especially need these to sell well. An author should negotiate for this support in the publishing contract. The best advice is to establish a good working relationship with one's editor and key personnel early and approach the project as a team effort.

There are differences in writing styles, language, and preparation of manuscripts in scholarly books versus textbooks. These differences are highlighted as the chapter progresses. Publishers generally supply a pamphlet or booklet describing their requirements. More about this later in the chapter.

Scholarly Books. The integrity of the writing is often based on the primary data offered as evidence. Data sources and references are of major importance to a reader. Careful attention to references, quotations, and citations is called for in this kind of work. Attention should be directed to ensuring that the overall manuscript reads as a book and not as a research report.

Dissertations to Books. As discussed in Chapter 2, the usual pitfall in converting a dissertation to a book is a failure to "de-research" the work. The manuscript may open with a chapter which introduces the overall framework, major research focus, purpose and need for the work, study methodology, and outline or overview of the rest of the book.

Each chapter following the introduction then presents its unique contributions to the overall theme of the book. Finally, the last chapters synthesize the ideas presented in the work. A bibliography is essential in a scholarly book and should follow the guidelines presented in Chapter 4.

Textbooks. A college text, while researched and planned much as a scholarly book is, does not focus on research in the same way. The overall purpose of a college text is to support the teaching and learning of a particular subject. An author's focus must be on accuracy of information, completeness, readability, clarity, and organization. Extensive references and citations are not as important in information presentation at the introductory level of text writing.

Writing Styles and Writing Tips

Clear language will attract a wider audience and make a work more enjoyable to read. Whether one seeks to write a scholarly book or a textbook, it is wise to be sensitive to a few potential problem areas faced by all writers.

Avoid wordiness. A publisher's contract will normally contain a page limit (see Chapter 8). Publishers incur additional expense and clarity suffers through verbosity. Maintain self-control when writing by sticking to the prospectus, avoiding tangents. Think through ideas and express them in direct language.

Define specialized terms. In both scholarly books and textbooks such terms can make reading difficult for the uninformed reader. Define each new term when you introduce it. Academic writers who use a specialized vocabulary for the sake of scientific accuracy should be alert to the danger of jargon.

Avoid excessive formality. While a certain aloofness is more tolerated in scholarly monographs where one expert is writing to another, a textbook which is colorless and impersonal is difficult to market. Use concrete words and the active voice whenever possible.

Day (1988) presents "The Ten Commandments of Good Writing" in the following spoof:

1. Each pronoun should agree with *their* antecedent.
2. Just between you and *I*, case is important.
3. A preposition is a poor word to end a sentence *with*.
4. Verbs *has* to agree with their subject.
5. Don't use *no* double negatives.
6. A writer *mustn't* shift your point of view.
7. When *dangling, don't* use participles.
8. Join clauses *good*, like a conjunction should.
9. Don't write a run-on sentence, it is difficult when you got to punctuate it so it makes sense when the reader reads what you wrote.
10. About sentence fragments. (p. 155)

Provide learning cues when writing a text. Organize the manuscript to help the readers learn the material more easily. This means using headings and sub-headings appropriately. Headings provide organizational structure for the work and allow readers to assimilate the material more readily. Keep headings consistent and parallel in construction. Highlight essential materials, ideas, or facts for the readers. Use illustrations, photographs, charts, diagrams, and other visual stimuli where they will enhance the written word and add clarity.

Textbook Writing—Additional Points

Be careful not to "date" a text needlessly. In history (or related political science) texts use of current events described in the present tense such as "during the current presidential campaign," soon dates the book. Current events should be discussed only in passing, and for illustrative purposes. Also be careful not to inject the time element into current history; be aware of phrases such as "since the resumption of Sino-Soviet relations." Perhaps, say instead, "After resumption of . . ." The best way to test for dating language is to proofread your manuscript as though it were five years later.

Be careful of sexist or other offensive language. While this is becoming less of a problem as more writers become sensitive, caution is still in order. Also, specifically guard against:

- unintentional slurs on race and religion, even indirect insulting language from such sources as quotations of others, poems, and references.
- broad criticisms or indictments of groups, such as professional groups, associations, unions, and industries.

COPYRIGHT ISSUES AND GUIDELINES

An often debated and perhaps misunderstood question posed by writers is how much information can be quoted from publications of others without written permission from the author or publisher. The Copyright Law of 1978 deals with the question in its interpretation of the issue of "fair use." *Fair use* of a copyrighted work is defined as use for the purpose of criticism, comment, news reporting, teaching, scholarship, or research.

The Copyright Law of 1978 also sets forth factors to be included in considering whether a particular use is fair. These include (1) the purpose and character of the use (i.e., is it commercial or for non-profit educational purposes?), (2) the kind of copyrighted work, (3) the amount and the substantiality of the amount used in relation to the entirety of the copyrighted work, and (4) the effect of the use on the potential market value of the copyrighted work.

The user bears final responsibility for all actions with respect to copyright violations. Therefore, authors must understand how this law applies to manuscript development. Guidelines vary from publisher to publisher, but many subscribe to the following guidelines.

1. When quoting from a copyrighted textbook, one may use up to 250 words (maximum) without permission except charts, tables, and materials to be used in anthologies. Be sure to credit the source. All quotations in excess of 250 words require written permission.
2. If the quotation is from a trade book (a book for the general public) obtain permission to use any quotation, whatever its length.
3. Obtain permission if the quotation exceeds 5 percent of the entire work from which it was taken.
4. If the quotation is poetry, no more than two lines should be used without permission, unless the two lines constitute a stanza; then a permission is required.
5. If it is a quotation to be used in an anthology or compilation, permission must be obtained for each selection in copyright.
6. If the material is from an unpublished work—a thesis, a lecture other than one's own, or material prepared by a student as part of a course—permission is needed.
7. If the quotation is from a letter that has been published under a copyright which has expired, no permission is necessary. But if it is protected by a copyright still in force, written permission to quote from it is needed.
8. If the quotation consists of music or lyrics which are protected by copyright, permission is needed.
9. Charts or tables need permission.
10. Plays, motion picture films, TV presentations and other copyrighted dramatic compositions need permission.

Speeches in the public domain may be freely copied without permission. Be careful, however, when quoting a speech in a newspaper or other news medium; this in and of itself does not place the speech in the public domain. Check for the original source.

Government documents and publications are themselves in the public domain. Generally speaking, U.S. government and state publications are not copyrightable. However, be sure material contained in these publications was not taken from other copyrighted material.

News as fact is not copyrightable, but news articles are. Permission must be obtained to quote feature stories, editorials, and syndicated columns, and to reproduce whole pages as specimens of newspaper format, and so on.

Likewise, all illustrations, graphics, and artwork taken from books, newspapers, and so forth, must have permission secured to be used.

Rights to translations of a work must be checked to ensure that permission is obtained from the rightful owner of the original work. Be aware that the English-language rights may be owned by someone other than the holder of rights to the foreign translations of the same work.

If you determine that the owner of a particular copyright is deceased, contact the estate of the copyright holder. This can be done by writing to the Library of Congress, U.S. Copyright Office, Reference and Bibliography Section, 101 Independence Avenue, SE, Washington, DC, 20559, requesting information about the deceased author's heirs. There is a fee for this service; the Copyright Office specifies the particular research costs.

The U.S. Copyright Office can also provide information about the holder of copyright of a particular work, when one is doubtful about a particular work.

Be sure to follow the style specified for credit lines by copyright permission grants.

Allow adequate time for publisher action—at least three months. Address copyright permissions requests to the publisher—not the author. The publisher will advise of any other requirements, or whether it is not the correct source to ask for permission.

Securing Copyright Holder's Permission

The U.S. District Court ruling in the case of *Basic Books v. Kinkos Graphics Corporation* shed new light on copyright issues. As a result, more and more academics and institutions have focused on securing permission to use copyrighted material developing any text material either for academic publishing or for general classroom use.

Requests should be made as follows (also see Chapter 4):

Give the publisher all of the information necessary—the exact wording of quotes, pages of text (including editions and year), illustrations (include photocopies of the pages), the name of the author(s), the ISBN, and so on.

Specify how the text is to be used—your publisher, hardcover or softcover edition, estimated printing, estimated number of pages, price, English or other language, and so on.

Give your name, address(es), contact telephone number, fax number, publisher name and address, and points of contact.

Tell the publisher who will pay for permissions, author or publisher.

Be aware of a new service for academics who do not wish to deal directly with publishers. For development of college course materials, they can contact The Anthologies Permission Service of the Copyright Clearance Center, at 27 Congress Street, in Salem, Massachusetts, 01970.

In summary, authors do not need permission to use the following:

1. U.S. government documents

2. U.S., state, court, and local government documents except those bearing a copyright notice

3. The original reprinted text of a classic—but not recent translations, edited text, or introductions, which are usually copyrighted

4. Unpublished materials, except archival manuscripts and letters of note that are controlled by organizations, families, or heirs

5. Books, articles, and pamphlets in which copyright notices have expired (in the United States copyright has expired on all works published prior to 1914)

Other Issues Relating to Copyright

Under Copyright. Written permission is obviously needed for use of quoted material in excess of fair use of works protected by copyright. United States copyright law now protects a work registered after January 1, 1978, for the lifetime of the author(s) plus fifty years. This follows the example of copyright law in the United Kingdom and Commonwealth countries. "Author" covers corporate authors, journals, associations, and so on. As a result of the new copyright law, a work registered before January 1, 1978, is still under statutory copyright protection if its registration was validly renewed. The copyright law protects such works for a maximum period of seventy-five years; specific cases vary, depending on the date of the original twenty-eight-year span of the statutory copyright and its renewal period (which was changed in 1978 from twenty-eight to forty-seven years). Full and up-to-date information about copyright can be obtained by writing to the United States Copyright Office.

Courtesy Permissions. Authors must obtain permission from their original publisher to use their earlier published work if the quoted material exceeds fair usage. Although the original publication may be copyrighted in an author's name, the publisher normally is responsible for release/permissions rights.

Permission Procedures. Publishers may require that the permission requested cover worldwide distribution and multiple printings of the work. Consider permission for paperback editions (along with the hardcover edition), if that is a factor, and publication in all necessary languages. If for any reason permission to reprint is withheld, it is best to delete or rewrite the material in question.

An editor will double-check an author's permissions. It is essential that the author send along a permission file with the completed manuscript. This includes a copy of the letter to each copyright holder (see Chapter 5, Figure 5-1, for sample letter) and a reply that gives full details about the exact wording that may be required in citing the material. As indicated earlier, copies of these letters are needed before the work is accepted for publication. Authors are also asked to compile a draft list of copyright acknowledgments that will appear on the copyright page. (Ordinarily, acknowledgments for illustrations appear only at the bottom of the illustration and not on the copyright page.)

MANUSCRIPT PREPARATION

The following are general guidelines for the preparation of manuscripts for both scholarly and college texts. The differences in preparation of scholarly book manuscripts from that of college text manuscripts are highlighted. Note that a good book begins with a well-written and well-prepared manuscript. The book must be conceptually sound as well as appealing and authentic.

Style

There are differences in the manner in which scholarly books are prepared stylistically. Consult the editor before preparing the final copy so that all agree on style and format for the text, notes, bibliography, appendices, and tables. There are several different styles used in academic publishing.

- *The Chicago Manual of Style*. Editorial Staff of the University of Chicago Press, 13th ed. (Chicago: The University of Chicago Press, 1982).
- *MLA Style Manual*, Walter S. Achtert and Joseph Gibaldi (New York: Modern Language Association, 1985).
- *Publication Manual of the American Psychological Association*, 3rd ed. (Washington, DC: American Psychological Association, 1984).

Other professional groups and organizations may subscribe to other styles, for instance, government sponsored publications use the *Government Printing Office (GPO) Style Manual*. Legal works use *A Uniform System of Citation*, Thirteenth Edition (Cambridge, Mass: The Harvard Law Review Association, 1981).

For textbooks, citations and bibliography styles are generally less critical than readability and technical accuracy. Therefore, publishers are not overly concerned with style manual specifications. Hence, a general agreement between author and publisher on style usually sets the stylistic guidelines.

Text

The manner in which text is prepared also differs for scholarly and text manuscripts. Today as a result of costs of printing and typesetting, some academic publishers are requiring camera-ready copy as final copy from authors. They usually require a text to be formatted single-spaced with one space between paragraphs for readability purposes.

Obtain a specification sheet detailing a publisher's needs and requests. Generally, double-spaced text is requested when the publisher intends to typeset copy, with 1.5 inch margins, top and bottom. Additional specifications for chapter heads, levels of sub-headings, quotation style, sequential page numbering, chapter notes, and the like, should be noted and followed.

Take particular note of such items as the following:

1. Folios are page numbers, placed on chapter interior pages in alternating right-left top margins and used consecutively.

2. Pagination of title pages, dedication page, acknowledgments, table of contents, foreword, preface, and introduction, which generally use roman numerals.

3. Footnotes, which vary with stylistic requirements and which are not used in text manuscripts. Generally, a quotation or material extracted from another source is set off with quotation marks, or, if it exceeds five lines of type, is set off from the surrounding text in indented form and single-spaced, with the source and page number immediately after the last word of quoted material.

4. Running heads, which are used in both academic and text manuscripts, are either book title or chapter title and are placed on the top line of the page. Style varies from publisher to publisher.

5. Illustrations and graphics, which are usually tables in academic manuscripts, are embedded in the text and developed according to the stylistic requirements. They may be line drawings, pictorials, or photographs in textbooks. They are usually put into final form and placed in the book according to readability and page layout by the publisher.

Tables are prepared and placed within the manuscript in a scholarly book. They are numbered consecutively throughout the book, and a list of tables follows the table of contents. Figures are noted in the manuscript, as are captions, but they are prepared separately as artwork for the publisher to cut into the final manuscript for both texts and scholarly books. Manuscript content determines costs and responsibilities for graphics preparation. Photographs are usually black and white glossy for production purposes. Label them on the back carefully for the printer, and include captions corresponding to the picture labels in the manuscript. The same holds true for any other artwork. The inclusion of an illustration in a manuscript is indicated by a figure caption insert box such as the following:

Insert Figure 1 about here

This illustration is placed at the point in the manuscript where you would like the illustration to appear.

6. Index. An index is generally required in both academic and college texts. The contract will specify who is responsible for its preparation.

Some other manuscript considerations an author should think about are discussed in the following sections:

Multiple Authorship. While not much has been said about multiple authorship, certain concerns need to be addressed. First, at the outset of your project establish responsibilities and communication protocols for the project's development. One of the authors in a multiple authored project should be designated as the spokesperson, or senior author, or simply publisher-interface person. This person should be given the authority to resolve any problems or make decisions about manuscript development and project administration. In any event, the process by which such decisions will be made should be agreed upon early in the project.

Inclusion of Learner Aids. Elements of a textbook such as end of chapter questions, activities for the learner, or suggested further readings all help readers to master the information by allowing them to apply what they have read. Be sure to have accurate questions and well explained exercises. Accuracy is very important.

Glossaries. Glossaries define specialized terms very precisely. They ensure that your reader understands the way in which language is used in the text. Glossaries are good inclusions in texts where technical language is used.

Footnotes or Endnotes. Often used in scholarly books, footnotes or endnotes allow the author to credit original sources or provide clarifications to the text material. Styles for footnotes or endnotes can be found in *The Chicago Manual of Style*.

Appendices. Supplementary information, charts, reference documents, and the like, are placed in an appendix in both scholarly books and textbooks.

EDITING THE MANUSCRIPT

The process of working with the publisher and editor in publishing a manuscript varies among publishers and differs in scholarly and textbook projects. The ultimate objective is to produce a high-quality product which will reflect the integrity of the subject material, appear attractive to the potential reader, and read well. This editorial process is a joint effort of the writer and the editorial staff.

A Typical Process

Authors may very well share earlier portions of the manuscript with their editor for intermediate comment and guidance; however, certain types of editorial activity do not begin until the final manuscript is delivered. A project editor looks over the final manuscript and determines its acceptability as a finished product.

Textbook Reviews. There are two kinds of reviews that a textbook will receive: a content review and an editorial review. A *content review* is intended to ensure content accuracy—a basic necessity for a text. Publishers often hire outside readers, peer reviewers who are experts in their respective fields, to do these reviews. The purpose is to ensure that nothing is missed or misinterpreted.

Once a content review is done, the project editor evaluates the various comments. The editor contacts the author and discusses the cumulative findings. Ideally, no major differences of opinion will emerge. One must, however, approach this task with an open mind and be prepared to compromise in certain areas or defend a point about which you feel strongly. A textbook is not a scholarly book. Philosophical issues, new theories, and/or controversial opinions do well in scholarly books; texts must be marketed to a wide and diverse student market. They must be contemporary and factual.

At the content review stage an author is also asked to check all references, quotes, and citations and be sure to obtain any copyright permissions needed. Remember, the editor is on the author's side and wants the book to succeed. One must detach personal vanity from the process.

An *editorial review*, which follows rewrites based on the content review, deals with issues of writing style, tone, organization of content, readability, and reader understanding. A publisher's in-house staff editor does this work. The first stage editorial review identifies a need for any large-scale reorganization and rewrite.

An author's task in this effort is to work with the editor's staff on inconsistencies in terminology or references (e.g., *learner* versus *student*). Sometimes the need to use more graphics or more examples can also be uncovered during editorial reviews.

Copyediting is done after any editorial review problems are resolved. A copy editor is assigned to go over the manuscript word by word, sentence by sentence, checking for grammar, spelling, awkward phrasing, stylistic inconsistencies, and overall quality of presentation. Depending on whether the work is a scholarly book or text, the copy editor focuses on the reader's point of view. If it is a text, the editor will work through a student's eyes.

It is essential to work closely with the copy editor. Larger publishing firms have copy editors working on a number of projects at the same time. Therefore, be sure to get all suggestions for changes in writing. Do not rely on telephone conversations.

The project's acquisitions editor corresponds with the author regarding any problems or concerns which surface as a result of these various reviews. At this point, text publishers convene a production staff meeting of copy editor, production editor, designer, illustrator, and marketing people to plan final production work. It is essential that the author work closely with those now involved with the project. The copy editor should thoroughly mark your manuscript and return it to you with questions. Standard editing marks are contained in various style manuals. Authors should communicate general suggestions or concerns about the edited manuscript to the production editor.

Editing a Marked Manuscript

An author's job is to address each of the concerns highlighted by the copy editor. In addition to marks, editors append notes to pages with specific questions or comments. Address each of these.

Work through the entire manuscript, addressing each comment, question, change, or misuse of word or structure. In camera-ready projects this is delivered according to template instructions. After a specified period the editor sends the proofs back to the author for a final reading.

The Proof Stage. Care in proofreading is essential. This is the last opportunity to make corrections and/or catch problems. Do not make arbitrary stylistic changes.

Use the standard editing marks to indicate problems which you uncover. Mark in red ink. Clearly mark any problems you find. Read the proofs against your final manuscript copy. Have an assistant read the manuscript as you follow on the proof. This is the most simple and accurate way to proofread.

Specifically, check for

- Typographical errors
- Omissions of text or words
- Sequential page numbering, figure numbering, footnote numbering
- Correct headings and sub-heads
- Illustration accuracy
- Cross-reference accuracy
- Copyright permissions (check that all have been received).

These suggestions will make your publication efforts easier and ideally more productive. In Chapter 10, the elementary and high school textbook publishing market is discussed. Many of the essentials discussed in these preceding chapters apply to EL-HI books. As will be seen in Chapter 10, however, there are some other important developmental considerations worth noting.

REFERENCES

Achtert, W. S., & Gibaldi, J. (1985). *MLA Style Manual*. New York: Modern Language Association.

The Association of American University Presses Directory, 1990–1991. (1990). New York: Association of American University Presses.

The Chicago manual of style. 13th edition. (1982). Chicago, IL: The University of Chicago Press.

Day, R. A. (1988). *How to write and publish a scientific paper*, 3rd edition. Phoenix, AZ: The Oryx Press.

GPO style manual. Washington, DC: U.S. Government Printing Office.

Prentice-Hall author's guide, 5th ed. (1978). Englewood Cliffs, NJ: Prentice Hall.

Publication manual of the American Psychological Association, 3rd edition. (1989). Washington, DC: American Psychological Association.

A uniform system of citation, 13th Edition. (1981). Cambridge, Mass: The Harvard Law Review Association.

Chapter 10

Book Publication—Phase II: Developmental Considerations for EL-HI Texts

Writing elementary and secondary textbooks can be both professionally rewarding and well compensated. Depending on the subject or discipline, the works can also be considered very acceptable academic accomplishments. EL-HI publishing entails many of the same skills and considerations discussed in the preceding chapters for college texts and scholarly works. It also requires a knowledge of instructional systems materials development (ISD) processes which will be discussed herein.

EL-HI publishing projects offer a publisher tremendous financial potential if the book is adopted by large central school districts or is included in a state education department approved textbook list. The units sold of a particular volume can reach into the many thousands. Publishers look for author (or author team) authority. Authors usually are experts in a field—or, if junior authors, become part of a recognized team.

Sometimes individual chapters or parts of an EL-HI project are contracted to outside writer(s) by the publisher. This is a way for writers who have published relatively little work to become involved in text writing. Additional development issues are discussed throughout the chapter, but first let's look at how the overall text project is developed.

BEGINNING THE EL-HI PROJECT

EL-HI educational materials, including textbooks, instructional software, computer programs, interactive disks, video-based media, and related learning materials, are best developed by a systematic development process. This ensures that the work reflects an overall high degree of quality and integrity. This process, better known as the instructional development process (ISD), guides overall writing development in five distinct phases. The ISD model (see Figure 10-1) provides an author a framework for the various product design considerations, including (1) guidelines for determining appropriate instructional media for the EL-HI learner (e.g., a text and/or computer-based software) and decisions about the learning environment (e.g., self-study materials or classroom-based materials); (2) actual step-by-step processes for materials development; (3) procedures for introducing the instructional products or materials to the intended audience; and (4) processes evaluating instructional materials or products, addressing the all-important question of whether the materials actually promote the goals of the text product, hence the educational process, and meet all of their instructional objectives.

PRODUCT NEEDS ANALYSES

Phase I of the ISD process is called the *analysis phase* (see Figure 10-2). It permits an author to identify the specific content to be included in the book and related materials. A content analysis addresses the specific details to be presented, discussed, and described to the reader audience.

Very often EL-HI review teams consisting of editors, content experts, and outside writers provide some of this input. Alternatively, individual portions of the book can be contracted out to content experts for development. It is imperative to be all-inclusive in the content analysis of the book. Ultimately the book will not sell well if teachers detect gaps or discrepancies with the accepted body of knowledge in a field. A concise and detailed outline of the book's content is the output of Phase I of the development process.

PRODUCT DESIGN

Phase II is the *design phase* (see Figure 10-3), which is a vital part of an EL-HI project. In Phase II the author identifies what the book should look like, in terms of layout, language, detail, tone, reading level, illustration

Figure 10-1
The Instructional Development Model

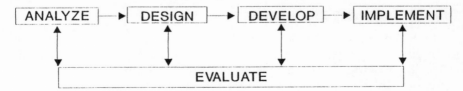

Figure 10-2
The Analysis Phase

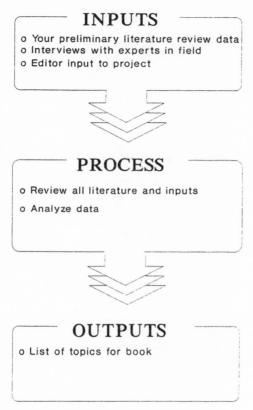

usage, exercises and activities, software accompaniment, and color scheme. Phase II decision making should actually begin in the pre-contractual phase of the book's development, although some of it may not occur until later in the project.

Part of Phase II involves matters relating to one's audience. For instance, an audience analysis will quickly reveal that the demographics of the U.S. student population is changing. A book writing project begun today will probably not be on the market for several years, at which time the typical American classroom will undoubtedly be more multi-lingual, multi-cultural, and multi-racial, with varying degrees of learning-related problems. What does this mean for a writing project?

First, it means that an author needs to be very sensitive to the various issues of cultural interpretations of political and historical events; to

Figure 10-3
The Design Phase

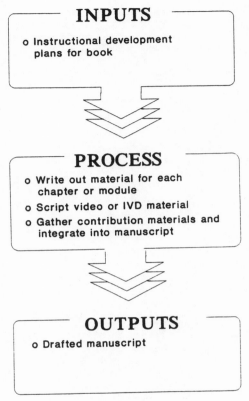

inadvertent stereotyping of peoples, cultures, and roles; to uses of appropriate language; to uses of terminology; to writing styles and reading levels appropriate to the audience; and to use of graphics and illustrations which complement the text and are not offensive to readers. Writing a textbook is no longer a simple exercise of putting fact onto page.

Phase II also facilitates decision making regarding appropriate instructional alternatives to accompany the text. A publisher can no longer produce a textbook without planning for the accompanying "bells and whistles," including exercises and activities—perhaps on a computer disk and/or in interactive videodisk. For instance, some science textbooks permit students to apply concepts discussed in the text materials visually via interactive and computer-based technology. Many teachers recognize that "learning via multi-sensory stimulation" is very effective—especially when a student can learn by doing—or applying concepts, rules, and ideas to situations which have meaning to him or her.

If the text development team decides to develop multi-media materials for the text, an author will need to develop some computer programming expertise. Usually a developmental editor can provide advice in this area. An author who can supply his or her own staff for the project probably will do better with writing coordination as well as negotiation of royalties.

There are optimal ways to lay out a manuscript to ensure that the learner will use the product successfully and thus receive the information. To begin, detail the specific factual information from Phase I which will be included in the book. Do not worry at this point about names and numbers of chapters. These will change as planning, layout, and writing revisions take place. Place the topics in logical groups; write learning objectives for each instructional topic; sequence the objectives and material for logical presentation and discussion. As this is done one will need to think about how any software used is to be integrated into the text (i.e., will all information be presented in the text, or will some be taught via the computer or videodisk?).

The final output of Phase II is a series of topical outlines (roadmaps of a sort), sequenced objectives, and factual information from which the text material will actually be drafted in Phase III.

PRODUCT DEVELOPMENT

Phase III is the *development phase* of this systematic process (see Figure 10-4). In Phase III an author is guided through the actual writing and mechanical preparation of the manuscript. Each piece or segment of the project (as mapped out in Phase II) is written, reviewed, and critiqued by the authors and others.

Authors should always keep readers in mind, as well as any language or learning problems which might be present in the typical population to which the authors are aiming. How does one go about this? There are various techniques EL-HI experts use to ensure audience acceptance of the text.

Reading level is very important in EL-HI materials. Become familiar with tools for checking reading level of materials, such as the FLEISCH-KINCADE Readability Formula. The formula permits writers to check text reading level by analyzing numbers of words on a line and syllables in a group of sentences.

Work with the editor on the design of illustrations and related graphics, so as to ensure that they are appropriate for the reading level.

In Phase III, the first draft of the manuscript in its proposed format is produced. Once all of the materials are drafted, Phase III also provides for a formative evaluation of the materials' effectiveness and consistency with the project's goals and objectives. The formative evaluation is a three-step

Figure 10-4
The Development Phase

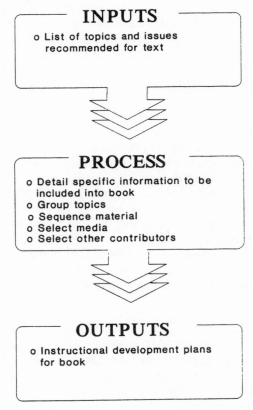

INPUTS

o List of topics and issues
  recommended for text

PROCESS

o Detail specific information to be
  included into book
o Group topics
o Sequence material
o Select media
o Select other contributors

OUTPUTS

o Instructional development plans
  for book

process. Step One begins with a one-on-one review in which the author identifies, selects, and meets individually with about three typical readers (learners) for whom the book is aimed. These learners are then asked to read through the text together with the author, in order to determine the following:

1. How well the material is drafted
2. How readable it is for this typical learner
3. Where any problems exist
4. Where any typographical errors exist
5. How well graphics are received
6. How well exercises or activities are interpreted and received

If any software has been developed to accompany the text, the author may also attempt to obtain feedback on it, even if it is only proofreading a storyboard script. At this point, it is also wise to subject the project materials, including text manuscript, to a technical content analysis, in a peer review by subject matter experts. This will ensure the material's content accuracy. Now compile the findings and decide what, if any, revisions need to be made to the manuscript materials. Make these changes.

At this point the author is ready to assemble the product into a pilot version. The publisher's project or developmental editor determines how the product should be packaged for a Step Two process review.

REVIEW MATERIALS

A Step Two process developmental review is made before an instructional product, such as an EL-HI textbook and/or instructional software, is completed to ensure that it meets its intended instructional objectives. Once it passes a Step Two review, the product is ready to go to the printer. Therefore, at Step Two the manuscript is assembled to look as much like the finished product as possible, but it should still be in a prototype stage of development.

For the Step Two review, the developmental editor and author together can identify a school (or other organization) that has a sufficient number of learners who fit the description of the target audience. With requisite permissions secured and cooperation provided by the host, the materials are used for a trial period. This corresponds to Phase IV, the *implementation phase* of the instructional development model (see Figure 10-5). Concurrent with the piloting, authors can develop any instructor guides, testing materials, or other supporting materials planned to supplement the text for eventual classroom adoption.

A Step Two review can take from three months to a full school year. The ultimate decision about readiness to proceed to complete the product must be based on the product's acceptability to the learners, the degree of cooperation extended by the host organization, and the complexity of the supporting software and/or materials. However, the longer the pilot, the more useful and reliable the data will be. Note, however, that the development of the supporting instructor guides and classroom materials is very important to the use and marketing of the text package. Authors should pilot these materials as well.

Consider the data gained from the Step Two developmental process review. Make whatever changes appear to be indicated. Discuss any major stylistic or format changes with the project editorial staff and the developmental editors. Sometimes format changes can be complicated and costly. Once a decision is made and the changes incorporated, the product is ready for printing and marketing.

Figure 10-5
The Implementation Phase

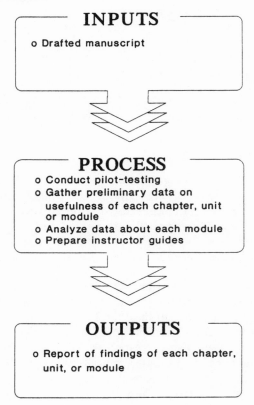

INPUTS

o Drafted manuscript

PROCESS

o Conduct pilot-testing
o Gather preliminary data on
   usefulness of each chapter, unit
   or module
o Analyze data about each module
o Prepare instructor guides

OUTPUTS

o Report of findings of each chapter,
   unit, or module

FINAL PRODUCT EVALUATION

Step Three of the developmental review process parallels Phase V of the instructional development model (see Figure 10-6). It is an overall evaluation of the product during its initial use. The entire development team as well as the publisher need to stay close to those teachers who adopt the text, to learn of its acceptance, problems found, or suggestions for future revisions. These comments can be considered for future printing or revisions (also see Chapter 11).

MULTI-AUTHOR WORKS

Multi-author projects are not easy to coordinate. EL-HI or college texts involving multiple authors, or reference books, special editions of a journal, and specialized monographs present challenges of a similar nature.

Figure 10-6
The Evaluation Phase

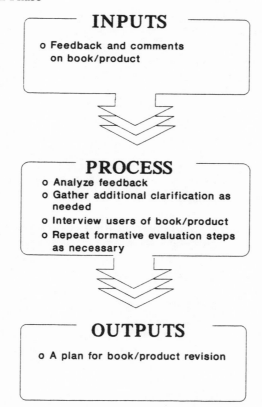

INPUTS

o Feedback and comments
  on book/product

PROCESS

o Analyze feedback
o Gather additional clarification as
  needed
o Interview users of book/product
o Repeat formative evaluation steps
  as necessary

OUTPUTS

o A plan for book/product revision

Working with Co-authors

Close collaboration of co-authors is essential to a multi-authored book's eventual completion. If co-authors are involved, establish writing responsibilities and goals carefully, and stay with them. In addition to the publishing contract, a written agreement which specifies responsibilities, deadlines, and procedures to deal with inability to comply is useful and should be considered. In this way if a project team member cannot meet his or her obligations, the project is not stalled indefinitely.

Projects also result from sponsorship of an association or professional society. These projects can be very worthwhile academic activities.

First and foremost, the number one frustration that the developer of such a project often faces is the interaction with multiple personalities, egos, and temperaments and thus the potential for disagreements on how the project should be developed. Selection of co-authors/contributors should be done most judiciously. The ultimate success of the project depends on (1) the substance and quality of the contributions and the expertise of the contributors, (2) the project editor's or lead author's ability to motivate each contributor to complete the project on schedule and to a desired level of quality, and (3) the editor's or author's ability to work with each contributor to ensure that manuscripts complement each other and the overall product. There are concerns of coverage, consistency, and perspective.

How then can one succeed in these kinds of projects? Once an editor has developed the theme to the point of knowing the objectives and kind of publication (book, monograph, special journal edition), the individual should identify potential authors/contributors who would be desirable collaborators. Contact with each should follow to determine individual interest. It is wise to identify more contributors than one actually will include, as more often than not some of the people initially contacted will not participate.

Develop a commitment letter outlining the goal of the project, the topic(s) that the author/contributor will write on; typical length requirements; style for manuscript preparation plus disk word processing requirements, if any; and deadlines. Also specify responsibilities for securing permissions for use of copyrighted material if the author/contributor will be responsible for doing so. Correspond with and get written commitments from each person who will participate.

Once the development period begins, monitor the contributors to ensure that each person is on schedule. Circulate the relevant chapters among the participants.

As manuscripts are finally delivered, begin editing them. As an editor or originator of the project you will assume primary editing responsibility. The editorial process is a major part of the project effort. One may be faced with an author's ego, which can make editing difficult, or with differences of opinion between a contributor and the editor and publisher. Resolution of these differences will be necessary if one wishes the project to survive.

Make sure to get requisite copyright releases from each contributor and permission secured by each contributor. If the manuscript is to be delivered in electronic format, one will also need to assemble, format, and compile a disk containing all of the manuscripts for final delivery to the publisher.

Anthologies

A similar kind of compiled multi-author text is the anthology. The difference here, however, is that an anthology is a collection of papers or articles which have been previously published. Very often anthologies are compiled for teaching purposes (when they are sometimes called readers).

An anthology to be used as a class project can be assembled and bound by the author, or it can be printed by a commercial printer. Permissions can be secured through the Anthology Clearinghouse (discussed in Chapter 7).

The major tasks to be undertaken in compiling an anthology are (1) selecting the pieces you wish to include in the work; (2) deciding how to present them in the book—in their original form (or retyped) and/or annotated and/or edited; (3) securing permissions for each work; and (4) preparing the final manuscript.

A WORD ABOUT INTELLECTUAL PROPERTY

Intellectual property is a concept that encompasses copyrights, trademarks, semi-conductor chip production, and technical data or know-how. These are protected by law from unauthorized use by others.

A fundamental understanding of intellectual property is essential to the academic writer; misunderstanding can have serious long-term consequences for author productivity, financial gain, and, above all, rights to claim ownership of ideas and inventions. Therefore, as stated by Mingle (1986), ''by planning ahead, faculty researchers can both publish their results and protect intellectual property rights'' (p. 262). The time to be aware of the pitfalls and potential problems in protecting one's copyright is when publication occurs.

What are some of the concerns? First, under what circumstances can one's intellectual property rights be challenged? Challenges can arise from (1) a university claim for financial gain and patent rights or copyrights from your invention, (2) an author's graduate student's potential rights to some portion of property rights in a work, and (3) claims of readers of one's previously published papers who adopt or adapt ideas and take them ''one step further'' into financially gainful inventions.

Knowledge has become what physical labor once was—an individual's source of power and wealth. A fact of life is that information cannot be owned: only its manner of packaging or assembly and manner of delivery to others can be controlled. As Cleveland (1989) offers, ''knowledge isn't exchanged in a market but shared in a kind of commons'' (p. 10). Patent and copyright laws have attempted to balance such conflicting ideas, thus ensuring balanced debate and challenge. The challenge, as Cleveland portrays it, is between the distinction between the expression of ideas (i.e., information and facts) and their use in a particular context. While paper print media have posed many challenges to the courts and claimants, the newly emerging technological media have added new fuel to the controversy. Computer software, compact disks, computerized data bases, satellites, all make the application of the patent and copyright laws more complex.

The University as Employer

Authors need to be aware of the court decisions and interpretations of the Copyright Act of 1978 as they apply to academia. Gorman (1987) describes many of these issues. He argues that the essence of the concern is that a professor is viewed as an employee of an academic institution for the purposes of ownership of academic articles, books, and other creations. This interpretation has been supported by arguments made by several legal experts.

Here the Copyright Act is less than supportive of the protection of author-owner of copyright of academic works. The statute defines a "work made for hire" as one prepared by an employee within the scope of his or her employment. Hence, it is reasonable to argue that the university can claim copyright of such works and can use them as it wishes, without permission, and can make revisions if it so chooses. Gorman further argues that the academic may be treated as the copyright owner if the two parties (university and author) have a written agreement so stipulating. Why such a legal interpretation? Gorman's argument is based on the legal precept that while the immediate purpose of copyright is to protect authors, its ultimate purpose is to advance knowledge by preventing copyright owners from overly guarding the ideas and discoveries of their work.

Not everyone agrees with this interpretation. Lichtenstein (1992) argues that most scholarly journal articles do not fit the definition of works-made-for-hire under Section 101 of the Copyright Act. Therefore, an author retains copyright.

This legal concept can also apply to academic work conducted under a grant or contract to you as a professor based at your university. To compound this issue, many contracts, especially federal contracts, have provisions protecting the government's rights to data collected under that contract. Clauses on "technical data" in federal research contracts conflict with other contract provisions on copyrights and patents. In many instances, a provision requiring dedication in the public domain of copyrightable works (surrendering them to the public) may preclude any intellectual property protection. The government generally has "unlimited rights" to technical data as created under contract.

And what about consultancies outside the university which may fit the works-for-hire definition, where compensation is received? These works produced for other employers are likely to belong to the employer; hence express agreements with the second employer are advisable. Familiarize yourself with the contractual particulars of your research vehicle, and how you may best protect your rights to publish.

Graduate Students as Research Partners. Ansell (1991) describes some of the issues surrounding graduate student participation in research activities. What rights and limitations does a graduate student have to research data for his or her continued research and publication use? The message here is to be aware of your immediate plans for your research findings or inventions and to exercise appropriate care in involving others in these works. Where necessary do the necessary legal paperwork to clarify the limitations of others' involvement in one's work.

Challenges from Others

Suppose you believe that another researcher has adopted or adapted part(s) of your work in a book, article, software invention, or device, which is then marketed or released under the other author's name. What courses of action or remedies does the current copyright law permit?

First, ascertain whether you are the rightful copyright holder. Then determine whether you in fact registered copyright to the particular writing, idea, or invention. You are obliged to place a copyright notice on your work when it has been published and distributed to the public. You need not place such a notice on the work to be protected—but it is wise to have the name of the copyright owner and the date the work is published on the document.

An issue often raised is fair use. It often serves as permission for certain unauthorized uses of copyrighted works that would promote the public interest and at the same time not excessively infringe on the copyright holder's prospects for economic rewards. The *Salinger v. Random House, Inc.* (811 F. 2nd 90 2nd Cir. 1987) case is a prime example of this doctrine in practice.

These comments are not intended to be an inclusive compilation of one's rights and responsibilities under existing copyright laws (i.e., intellectual property). Read more on the topic and consult counsel. Several useful sources of information are listed in the references section of this book.

SELF-PUBLISHING

Some authors who have published a text in the past have probably felt somewhat perturbed by the amount of work devoted to the project *versus* the royalties received. Many have wondered whether it would have been better to publish the work personally and thus perhaps reap bigger profits. Aside from the issue of scholarly recognition—which for tenured professors is of little concern perhaps—if one does not mind hard work and long hours one may decide to publish his or her own work.

Manuscripts need to be produced electronically, as described in Chapter 8. Therefore, good typing and editing are essential. Authors need to be able to do this or hire others to provide these services.

A very critical concern to a self-publisher is a printer-typesetter. There are several different ways to produce a book, ranging from photocopying to phototypesetting. Phototypesetting offers very high quality print. Laser typesetting closely resembles phototypesetting but costs much less. Once the manuscript is electronically ready, a printer can take the disk and transfer it electronically to the typesetting computer. Again, a hard copy manuscript submitted with the disk permits a printer to make a quality check to verify that the copy has been transferred properly.

Shop among several printing firms and discuss and compare quoted costs. Costs vary considerably and decrease per unit with the numbers of copies ordered. Generally, press runs of one thousand are used for quoting purposes. Discuss bindings—which also impact costs. Stitched *versus* glued *versus* perfectbound bindings are commonplace; as is hard *versus* soft cover. For texts, a soft cover helps to keep the retail price within reason.

Once the issues of printing are settled, the next concern is distribution. Considerations include where to stock the books and how to package, invoice, and fulfill orders as they are received. Book distribution firms can be contracted to provide all of these services. All one needs to do is use their ordering service as a customer-point-of-contact—whereby the customer is directed to place orders directly with them—or generate one's own sales and fax the orders directly to the distributor. You are, of course, generating costs in the process.

Advertising is the next challenge. Access to mailing lists is needed for all targeted markets. They can be bought. Prepare advertisements and flyers and do a targeted mailing. Consider advertisements in magazines, journals, or other professional media—all of which a publisher would pay for under standard arrangements.

A major cost item is giving free copies or examination copies to people in a position to adopt the book. Invoicing, billing, and collections are additional tasks to be performed. Self-publishing can be very costly. It requires knowledge and work, in addition to money, but is occasionally profitable.

REFERENCES

Ansell, E. O. (editor). (1991). *Intellectual property in academe: A legal compendium*. Washington, DC: National Association of College and University Attorneys.

Cleveland, H. (1989). How can intellectual property be protected? In Ansell, E. O. (editor). *Intellectual property in academe: A legal compendium*. Washington, DC: National Association of College and University Attorneys.

Gorman, R. A. (1987). Copyright and the professorate: A primer and some recent developments. In Ansell, E. O. (editor) (1991). *Intellectual property in academe: A legal compendium*. Washington, DC: National Association of College and University Attorneys.

Levine, M. L. (1988). *Negotiating a book contract: A guide for authors, agents, and lawyers*. Mt. Kisco, NY: Moyer, Bell.

Lichtenstein, A. (1992). To the editor. *Chronicle of Higher Education*, July 1, B-3.
Mingle, J. O. (1986). Patenting versus publication. In Ansell, E. O. (editor) (1991). *Intellectual property in academe: A legal compendium*. Washington, DC: National Association of College and University Attorneys.

Chapter 11

Book Publication—Phase III: Marketing

The ultimate success of a publication of any kind rests on its marketing—a key responsibility of the publisher. Yet very little appreciation of marketing appears to go into planning for marketing in the academic community. This is so for several reasons—the prime one being greater emphasis on tenure and promotion than on financial gain. Tenure and promotion considerations obviously need not exclude good marketing. Attention can be drawn to the merit of the book through better distribution achieved through good marketing plans. Larger publishing houses have well-established procedures for book marketing, but, like smaller firms, they welcome an author's input and suggestions. These activities are the focus of this chapter.

All books benefit from the sound execution of some basic marketing techniques. Among the more common techniques which an author should discuss with a publisher are (1) strategies for publicity and promotion, (2) commercial sales, (3) periodical-based advertising, (4) direct mail, (5) field sales personnel, (6) bibliographic sales, (7) exposure through professional conferences, and (8) professional book reviews.

PUBLICITY AND PROMOTION

Planning for publicity and promotion should be done well before the book galleys are prepared. Authors should think about the avenues which are most appropriate for the book and call the publisher's attention to them. If the project is a scholarly work, where are the academicians and others located who most likely will refer to and use it? Develop a list of names, addresses, and professional affiliations of those likely to be interested. Authors should review directories and association membership lists. Review past journals in the field for names of professional societies whose membership lists and newsletters can be accessed. Suggest the most appropriate professional journals and related media to the publisher. Very often a review in one or more of these media is a very good source of publicity for the book. For scholarly review some journals accept page proofs before the release of the book; others accept only bound books. It is, obviously, very important to get the book reviewed.

Review copies (sample or desk copies) of texts should be sent by the publisher to appropriate individuals for review for possible adoption (professors, school district administrators) and to professional organizations where adoption exposure can be gained. Authors should work closely with the marketing department to identify these appropriate individuals and organizations. A publisher's marketing staff often builds or purchases lists for these purposes. Association directories, state education department directories, and commercial lists are all useful for this purpose. Many publishers prepare a title's advanced publication information, including its title, series, author(s), price, ISBN, cataloging-in-publication data, publication date, and comprehensive descriptive information, all of which are mailed with the review copy to potential purchasers. Publishers should also prepare data for inclusion in promotional flyers, textbook catalogues, publicity releases, and the like.

Other kinds of publicity and promotion have proved useful for marketing.

Conventions and Exhibits

Text publishers regularly attend the larger national conventions such as that of the American Educational Research Association. Exhibitors at these functions have an opportunity to promote their new products to large numbers of specialized audiences. In the case of EL-HI texts, conventions of teachers and administrators can give large numbers of potential adopters the opportunity to look over a new text. An author's or editor's attendance at these functions can be beneficial if the purpose is well defined and activities are planned.

Some scholarly publishers also attend smaller conventions using the services of a cooperative book exhibit company. An author should ask or advise the publisher about appropriate opportunities for exhibiting his or her academic work.

Personal Appearances

Titles which are timely in terms of public interest very often can be promoted by using mass media—TV, radio, newspapers. Again, authors need to help the publisher to get the word out about their books.

Commercial Sales

Commercial sales include general domestic distribution, foreign distribution, distributions to wholesalers, and sales to bookstores. Authors generally do not have much input or involvement in these activities, but they should understand them. The publisher will fulfill orders directly or through a distributor who receives customer orders and ships books. Some publishers have agents overseas in London, India, Singapore, Tokyo, Australia, and Cyprus—covering much of the world.

Two of the major academic and professional wholesalers are Baker & Taylor and Blackwell North America. Such firms order quantities of selected books and distribute them to libraries and retail bookstores as their sales increase.

Scholarly books are generally not sold directly to retail bookstores; however, some bookstores that serve selected markets do buy appropriate scholarly titles. Sometimes an author can work with the publisher to develop a marketing plan for this kind of distribution system.

Finally, opportunities do exist for both scholarly books and textbooks to be included among the titles a publisher offers to book clubs, associations, and other mass merchandising avenues. Such books have to possess the appeal described earlier in Chapter 8. Authors should provide a publisher with the names of specialized organizations which are likely to offer great sales potential for the work.

Advertising

Scholarly book publishers work primarily through direct mail to reach markets. Text publishers are likely to use space advertising as well as direct mail and representative calls to reach a textbook's potential audience. Publishers work with authors to identify appropriate places to place ads—such as professional or trade journals, professional magazines, association publications, and professional newspapers (e.g., *The Chronicle of Higher Education*). Authors should give thought to those media and advise their publishers of their recommendations.

Direct Mail

All publishers regularly direct mass mail catalogs and flyers to college and university departments, and to public and special libraries. Text publishers also buy association mailing lists appropriate to the subject and audience of the text.

Many scholarly publishers also produce specialty subject catalogs such as women's studies, black studies, and military studies, and quarterly special subject catalogs such as social sciences (economics, political science, and history), humanities (religion, philosophy, literature, performing arts, and popular culture), behavioral sciences (sociology, psychology, health), and sub-sets of business and reference. These specialty catalogs are mailed to libraries and college professors.

Commercially available mailing lists of college faculty can be ordered by specific course areas. Similar kinds of lists of public school personnel and personnel in other disciplines are available. Mailings with descriptive literature and order forms for the product are also intended to generate sales. Likewise, texts which are good references for specific business and professional groups can be marketed to these groups by mail.

Bibliographic Sales

Many scholarly publishers rely heavily on bibliographic selling. This kind of marketing relies on ensuring that books are listed among the basic bibliographic tools that are used by book purchasers. Included are the data base of the Library of Congress; the *Weekly Record*, which is a title compilation by the Library of Congress; *Books in Print*; *Cumulative Book Index*; and the data bases of all major book wholesalers.

FOLLOWING PROGRESS

Authors should carefully review and critique the finished book. Look for typographical errors, broken type, and other possible flaws and prepare a list. If the book warrants a second printing, the errors should be in a reprint file and be corrected.

Seek feedback about the book from readers. If it is a text, they can provide data about the book's technical presentation, readability, balance, and deficiencies.

A successful textbook will need to be updated periodically. Authors must stay abreast of market changes and readership composition while maintaining integrity of content and approach.

New markets and opportunities will continue to challenge academicians.

REFERENCES

Books in print. Titles A–F, 4, (1990–1991). New York: R. R. Bowker.
Cumulative Book Index (1992). New York: H. W. Wilson.
U.S. Library of Congress. *Weekly Record*, Washington, DC.

References

Achtert, W. S., & Gibaldi, J. (1985). *MLA style manual*. New York: Modern Language Association.

Adams, M. R. (1989). Tenuring and promoting junior faculty. *Thought and Action*, Fall, 5(2), 35–60.

Adult Education Network (AEDNET). (1992). *New horizons in adult education*. Syracuse, NY: Syracuse University.

American Psychological Association. (1992). *PSYCOLOQUY*. Princeton, NJ: Princeton University.

Annual register of grant support, 1982–1983, 16th edition. (1992). Chicago: Marquis Professional Publications.

Ansell, E. O. (editor). (1991). *Intellectual property in academe: A legal compendium*. Washington, DC: National Association of College and University Attorneys.

Applied Science & Technology Index. (1990). New York: H. W. Wilson.

Article clearinghouse catalog. (1989). Ann Arbor, MI: University Microfilms International.

The Association of American University Presses Directory, 1990–1991. (1990). New York: Association of American University Presses.

Blum, D. E. (1991). Use of photocopied anthologies for courses snarled by delays and costs of copyright-permission process. *The Chronicle of Higher Education*, September 11, A19.

Blum, D. E. (1991). The path to publishing: An idea, a contract, maybe even royalties. *Chronicle of Higher Education*, July 31, A11.

Board of Higher Education of the City of New York. (1975). *Statement of the Board of Higher Education on academic personnel practice in the City University of New York*. New York: Board of Higher Education of the City of New York.

Books in print. Titles A–F, 4. (1990–1991). New York: R. R. Bowker.

Books in series in the U.S., 4th edition. (1985). New York: R. R. Bowker.

Bowker's complete video directory. (1992). New York: R. R. Bowker.

Boyes, W. J., Happel, S. K., and Hogan, T. D. (1984). Publish or Perish: Fact or Fiction? *Journal of Economics Education*, Spring, 136–141.

Buell, C. (1989). *Demands for research and publication at the small college*. Paper presentation at the Speech Communication Association Annual Convention, San Francisco, CA.

Business Periodicals Index. (1990). December, *33*(4).

Buzza, B. W. (1989). *Faculty perceptions of publication expectations in the small college setting: Have the rules changed?* Paper Presentation at the Convention of the Speech Communication Association, San Francisco, CA.

Cantor, J. A. (1992). *Delivering instruction to adult learners*. Toronto, Ontario, CAN: Wall & Emerson.

Center for Community College Education. (1989). *New horizons series in community colleges*. San Francisco: Jossey-Bass.

Cheney, L. V. (1990). Research and teaching: An excerpt from Cheney report on educational practices gone wrong. *The Chronicle of Higher Education*, November 14, *37*(9), A22, 24–26.

The Chicago manual of style, 13th edition. (1982). Chicago, IL: The University of Chicago Press.

Children's books in print. (1991–1992). New York: R. R. Bowker.

The Chronicle of Higher Education. (1991). Prentice-Hall plans to offer computer programs with 5 physics textbooks to allow simulations. *The Chronicle of Higher Education*, September 11, A-21.

The Chronicle of Higher Education. (1991). Annual events in academe. *The Chronicle of Higher Education*, August 15, p. 32.

Cleveland, H. (1989). How can intellectual property be protected? In Ansell, E. O. (editor) *Intellectual property in academe: A legal compendium*. Washington, DC: National Association of College and University Attorneys.

Coughlin, E. K. (1991). University presses ponder their role in a future clouded by financial and cultural upheaval. *The Chronicle of Higher Education*, July A5, A9.

Cumulative Book Index. (1992). New York: H. W. Wilson.

CUNY Faculty Development Program. (1990). *On publishing in the academia*. New York: New York Professional Staff Congress/CUNY.

Day, R. A. (1988). *How to write and publish a scientific paper*, 3rd edition. Phoenix, AZ: The Oryx Press.

Delton, J. (1985). *The 29 most common writing mistakes (and how to avoid them)*. Cincinnati, OH: Digest Books.

DeMinco, S. (1991). *The educational journal monitor*. New York: Lehman College.

DIALOG information retrieval service directory. (1983). Palo Alto, CA: Lockheed Missiles and Space Company.

Directory of electronic manuals, newsletters, and academic discussion lists. (1992). Washington, DC: Association of Research Libraries.

Directory of research grants. (1982). Phoenix, AZ: Oryx Press.

Eastern Educational Research Association. (1989). *Annual conference call for papers & symposia—1989*. Albany, NY.

Eastern Educational Research Association. (1991). *Newsletter of the Eastern Educational Research Association*, Summer, *4*(3). Oswego, NY.

Easton, T. A. (1983). *How to write a readable business report.* Homewood, IL: Dow Jones - Irwin.

Educational Index. (1990). December, *62*(4).

EL-HI textbooks and serials in print. (1991). New York: R. R. Bowker.

Encyclopedia of associations, 25th edition. (1991). Princeton, NJ: Gale Research.

Euster, G. L. & Weinbach, R. W. (1986). Deans' quality assessment of faculty publications for tenure and promotion decisions. *Journal of Social Work Education,* Fall, *22*(3), 79–84.

Forthcoming Books. (1991). August, *26*(4). New York: R. R. Bowker.

General guide for authors. (1989). Westport, CT: Greenwood Publishing Group.

Gorman, R. A. (1987). Copyright and the professoriate: A primer and some recent developments. In Ansell, E. O. (editor) (1991). *Intellectual property in academe: A legal compendium.* Washington, DC: National Association of College and University Attorneys.

Government Information Services. (1990). *Guide to federal funding for governments and non-profits.* Arlington, VA: James J. Marshall.

Haile, S. W. (1991). *Foundation Grants to Individuals,* 7th edition. New York: Foundation Center.

Hall, K. (1991). The publishing journey. *Training and Development,* August, 31–38.

Harvard graphics, version 2.3 (1990). Mountain View, CA: Software Publishing Company.

Henson, K. T. (1990). Writing for education journals. *Phi Delta Kappan,* June, 800–803.

Henson, K. T. (1987). *Writing for professional publication.* Bloomington, IN: Phi Delta Kappa Educational Foundation.

Koek, K. E., & Winklepleck, J. (editors). (1991). *Gale directory of publications and broadcast media: An annual guide to publications and broadcasting stations.* Detroit: Gale Research.

Levine, M. L. (1988). *Negotiating a book contract.* Mt. Kisco, NY: Moyer-Bell.

Lewis, M. O., & Teitz-Gersumsky, A. (editors). (1981). *The foundation directory,* 8th edition. New York: The Foundation Center.

Literary marketplace: The directory of the American book publishing industry. (1991). New York: R. R. Bowker.

Luey, B. (1990). *Handbook for academic authors.* Cambridge, England: Cambridge University Press.

Market, A., & Rinn, R. C. (1985). *Author's guide to journals in psychology, psychiatry, and social work.* New York: Haworth.

McShane, K., & Dovzenis, C. (1987). *Evaluation and reward: Is research the only way?* Paper presented at the Annual meeting of the Mid-South Educational Research Association, November, Mobile, AL.

Meador, R. (1986). *Guidelines for preparing proposals.* Chelsea, MI: Lewis Publishers.

Medical and health care books and serials in print. (1991). New York: R. R. Bowker.

Military Testing Association. (1992). *Abstract preparation for the annual conference of the Military Testing Association (MTA).*

Miller, A. R., & Davis, M. H. (1983). *Intellectual property: Patents, trademarks, and copyright in a nutshell.* St. Paul, MN: West Publishing.

Mingle, J. O. (1986). Patenting versus publication. In Ansell, E. O. (editor). (1991). *Intellectual property in academe: A legal compendium*. Washington, DC: National Association of College and University Attorneys.

National Information Service for Earthquake Engineering. (1990). *Abstract Journal in Earthquake Engineering*, Earthquake Engineering Research Center, April, 15(2).

Neff, G. T. (editor) (1990). *1990 Writer's market: Where & how to sell what you write*. Cincinnati: Writer's Digest Books.

New York Times. (1991). *Book Review Section*. January 22, cover.

1987 Gale Directory of Publications, 119th edition. (1987). Princeton, NJ: Gale Research.

1988 Yearbook of Vocational Education. (1988). Washington, DC: American Vocational Association.

Noble, K. A. (1989). Publish or perish: What 23 journal editors have to say. *Studies in Higher Education, 14*(1), 97–102.

On Cassette. (1992). New York: R. R. Bowker.

Online journal of current clinical trials. (1991). Washington, DC: American Association for the Advancement of Science.

Parsons, P. (1989). *Getting published: The acquisition process at university presses*. Knoxville: University of Tennessee Press.

Penaskovic, R. (1983). Facing up to the publication gun. *Scholarly Publishing*, January, 136–140.

Powell, W. W. (1985). *Getting into print: The decision-making process in scholarly publishing*. Chicago: University of Chicago Press.

Preparing your electronic manuscript. New York: Association of American University Presses.

Publication grants for writers and publishers. (1991). Phoenix, AZ: Oryx Press.

Publication manual of the American Psychological Association, 3rd edition. (1989). Washington, DC: American Psychological Association.

Publishing, distribution and wholesalers of the United States. (1992). New York: R. R. Bowker.

Religious and inspirational books and serials in print. (1987). New York: R. R. Bowker.

Schweitzer, J. C. (1989). Faculty research expectations vary among universities. *The Journalism Educator*, Summer, 44(2), 45–49.

Scientific and technical books and serials in print. (1992). New York: R. R. Bowker.

Serials in print (1991). New York: R. R. Bowker.

Sheridan, D., Richards, & Dowdney, D. L. (1986). *How to write and publish articles in nursing*. New York: Springer Publishing.

Shulman, C. (1979). *Old expectations, new realities: The academic profession revised* (AAHE/ERIC Higher Education Research Report No. 2). Washington, DC: American Association for Higher Education.

Simon, T. F. (1976). Faculty writings: Are they works made for hire? *Journal of College and University Law* 9(4), 1983, Under the 1976 COPYRIGHT ACT. In Ansell, E. O. (editor) (1991). *Intellectual property in academe: A legal compendium*. Washington, DC: National Association of College and University Attorneys.

Smith, P. (1990). *Killing the spirit: Higher education in America*. New York: Viking Penguin.

Social Sciences Index. (1990). December, 17(4).

Soderberg, L. O. (1985). Dominance of research and publication: An unrelenting tyranny. *College Teaching*, Fall, *33*(4), 168–172.

Software encyclopedia. (1991). New York: R. R. Bowker.

Subject guide to books in print. (1990). New York: R. R. Bowker.

Submitting documents to ERIC. Washington, DC: National Institute of Education.

Swinburne, L., & Bank, S. (1987). *Cloze: Stories for beginning readers, book one*. New York: Walker and Company.

Tennant-Neff, G. (editor). (1987). *The writer's essential desk reference*. Cincinnati, OH: Writers Digest Books.

Thomas, R. C., & Ruffner, J. A. (1982). *Research Centers Directory*, 7th edition. Detroit: Gale Research.

Training and Development Journal (editor). (1989). How to get your book published. *Training & Development Journal*, *44*, August, 17–24.

Ulrich's International Periodicals Directory, 27th edition. (1988–1989). New York: R. R. Bowker.

A uniform citation, 13th edition. (1981). Cambridge, MA: Harvard Law Review Association.

UPA Manuscript Preparation Guide. Lanham, MD: University Press of America.

U.S. Congress, Office of Technology Assessment. (1986). *Intellectual property rights in an age of electronics and information*. Washington, DC: U.S. Congress.

U.S. Department of Commerce, National Technical Information Service. (1990). *FEDIX: An on-line information service for universities and other research organizations: User's guide*. Washington, DC: U.S. Department of Commerce.

U.S. Department of Education, Office of Educational Research and Improvement (1986). *Directory of ERIC information service providers*. Washington, DC: U.S. Department of Education.

U.S. Department of Health and Human Services, K. Patrias (editor). (1987). *AIDS Bibliography, 1986–1987*. Washington, DC: National Library of Medicine.

U.S. Federal Emergency Management Agency. (1987). *Learning resource center user's guide*. Emittsburg, MD: U.S. Federal Emergency Management Agency.

U.S. Government Printing Office. (1985). *GPO style manual*. Washington, DC: U.S. Government Printing Office.

U.S. Library of Congress. *Weekly Record*, Washington, DC.

Van Leunen, M. (1992). *A handbook for scholars*. New York: Oxford University Press.

Watkins, B. T. (1991). San Diego campus and McGraw-Hill create custom texts. *The Chronicle of Higher Education*, 1991, *28*(2).

Wiersma, W. (1991). *Research methods in education*, 5th edition. Boston: Allyn & Bacon.

Wilson, D. L. (1991). New electronic journal to focus on research on medical treatments. *The Chronicle of Higher Education*, October 2, *38*(7), A-27.

Wilson, D. L. (1991). Researchers get direct access to huge data base. *The Chronicle of Higher Education*, October 2, *38*(7), A24-29.

WordPerfect, Version 5.1. (1989). Orem, UT: WordPerfect Corporation.

Index

About the Author

JEFFREY A. CANTOR is Associate Professor of Adult Education and Corporate Training, Lehman College, City University of New York. Among Professor Cantor's earlier book and journal publications is *A History of the Public Debt in the United States* (Praeger, 1989).